THE
COOK

AND
BAKER

CHERIE BEVAN · TASS TAUROA

THE
COOK

AND
BAKER

CHERIE BEVAN · TASS TAUROA

MURDOCH BOOKS

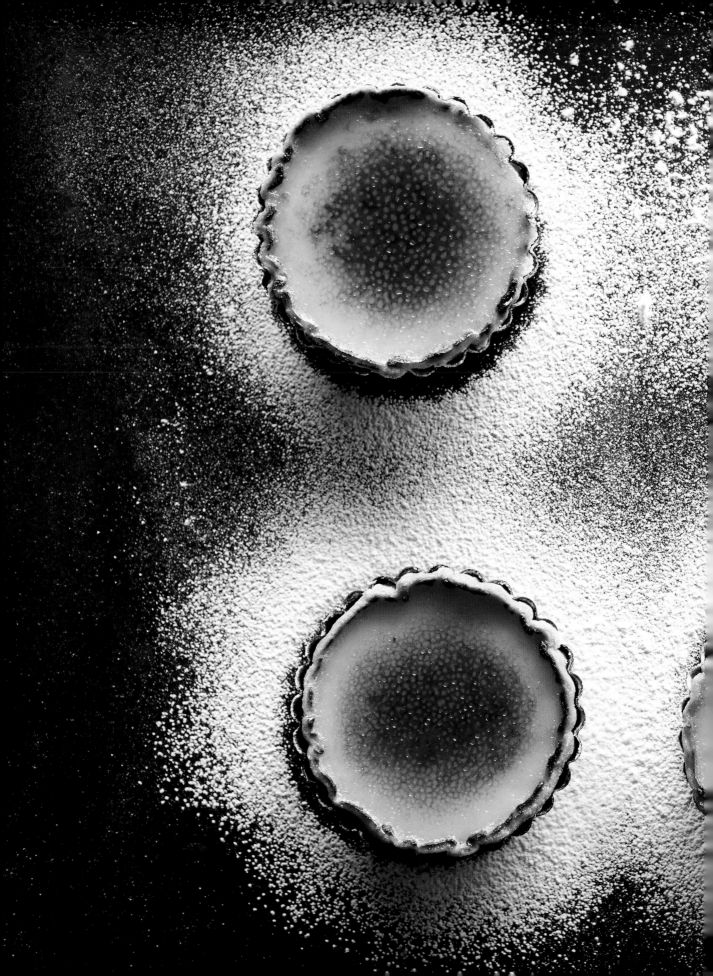

FOR OUR
MOTHERS,
RAWINIA
AND
CAROLYN

INTRODUCTION

When The Cook and Baker opened its doors in Sydney in August 2012, we weren't entirely certain how people would react. Diet gurus were preaching that 'sugar is poison'; and raw food, the Mediterranean diet and the joys of green juice were all the rage. In our Bondi Junction neighbourhood we had three organic health-food shops within a 500-metre radius. Was the world ready for the return of the big fat jam donut, the lolly cake and a ginger crunch modelled on our mothers' faded handwritten recipes from last century?

It didn't take long to find out. Some of our customers may have looked guilty as they ordered a cream-filled chocolate lamington with their latte in those opening weeks, but The Cook and Baker soon had crowds milling four-deep outside the shopfront. It turned out we weren't the only people who harboured a nostalgic longing for richly flavoured cooking.

In our case, that nostalgia has its roots in the home-baking traditions of New Zealand, where we both grew up. Despite our different backgrounds – Cherie was raised in suburban Auckland, Tass from Hunterville, a rural community of only 500 people – both of us remember the generous aromas and tastes emanating from the family kitchen as our induction into the shared pleasures of food. Cherie can recall spending hours baking cakes and pastries with her mother and Nana, who handwrote her recipes and collated them into Cherie's first cookbook. In Tass's case, food was intrinsic to the communal Maori culture he was born into: the traditional meeting place known as the *marae* was where hundreds of extended family members would congregate for birthdays, weddings and funerals – gatherings that required industrial-scale cooking and baking that stretched over several days. It was a training ground that stood Tass well during his early teens when he began working with an aunty who ran a catering business and offered Devonshire teas at her home.

The bible for home cooks In New Zealand was – and remains – the Edmonds *'Sure To Rise' Cookery Book*, a spiral-bound trove of recipes that includes such old-fashioned delicacies as Albert squares, sausage rolls, hokey-pokey biscuits and tennis cake. Many of these were homegrown adaptations of traditional English recipes, and they filled the window displays of the 'home-cookery' shops in every town and suburb. Mastering these baking traditions was part of our basic training as chefs.

Cherie left school at 14 to enrol in a cooking course at Auckland's Polytechnic College, and by 17 she was head chef at a successful delicatessen and catering business run by her early mentor and taskmaster, Christine Hall. Tass served his teenage apprenticeship in a Hunterville home-cookery business run by the sprightly seventy-something baker Joyce Flintoff, who taught him the culinary secrets of the Country Women's Institute. Tass also graduated from the Polytechnic, after joining the navy in his late teens, although his path wouldn't cross with Cherie's until 1994. That year Cherie moved to Sydney to start her own café and catering business, Gusto's, in Bondi, placing an advertisement for a chef in *The New Zealand Herald* (Sydney was suffering a chef shortage at the time). Tass answered the ad and flew to Sydney fresh from his discharge from the navy, where he had completed his service as personal chef to the Maritime Commander. He recalls stepping off the plane in Sydney and meeting Cherie in the kitchen of her new café, where she was elbow-deep in a vast bowl of olives that required pitting. The bond that formed that day was instant and enduring, shaped by a shared Kiwi irreverence and a strong work ethic. Tass started work the next day at 5 am sharp!

It's said you should never go into business with a close friend, but over 20 years of working together in several different food businesses we have forged such a simpatico relationship that becoming partners became a natural development. In 2012 we began talking about opening a store that filled a gap in the market of baking in the style we remembered from our family kitchens – food that was about generosity rather than the prevailing trend for self-denial. The idea was to modernise and refine those traditional recipes and to also stay true to the ideals of home-baking: source the best raw ingredients, avoid anything pre-packaged and try to make as much as possible in-house. In our minds, our shop would be an updated version of the old New Zealand home-cookery shops, selling irresistible pastries, whole cakes, pies and sandwiches, and using organic and locally grown ingredients as often as we could. Somewhere along the way, the idea developed that one of us would be the cook – Cherie – and the other the baker – Tass – and we had a name for our nascent venture.

Some of those traditional recipes, like the Afghan biscuit, the Louise cake and the custard tart proved to be immediate favourites with our customers. But with our gluten-free goods – the flourless mandarin marmalade cake, flourless chocolate fudge cake and raw brownie – we could cater to modern taste needs without sacrificing flavour and the sense of abundance that were our guiding principles. As much as possible, we have stuck to the ideal of home-made ingredients, from the jam in our donuts to the tomato sauce served with our pies and the honey from our rooftop hives.

In *The Cook and Baker* we hope to share the unalloyed pleasure from cooking that first enticed us into our family kitchens and set us on the path to becoming chefs. Some of the recipes come directly from our mothers and grandmothers. All of them contain at least a little of the wisdom and skill of those women who were our first mentors and teachers. We like to think they're looking down and giving us their blessing.

CHERIE AND TASS

CHERIE
BEVAN

TASS
TAUROA

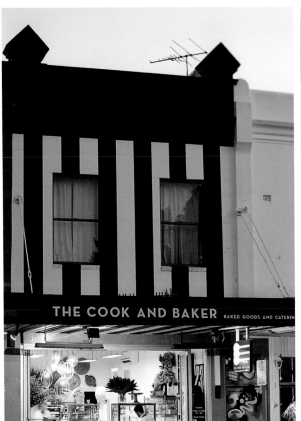

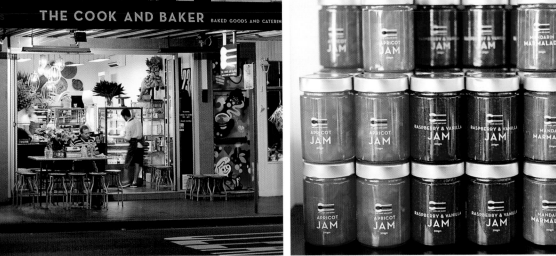

CAKES

The joy of baking is in the sharing.
We are not the kind of people to keep
recipes secret. Why, when so many
memories are shared over cake?
We love cake!!

We have all had cakes that promised actual chocolate flavour but didn't deliver. Unadorned, this cake is rich and moist, but layered with raspberry jam, whipped cream and a smooth, creamy chocolate ganache, this one takes the cake!

CHOCOLATE GANACHE CAKE, BERRY JAM AND CREAM

Serves 10–12 • **Makes** one 23 cm round cake • **Preparation time** 1 hour • **Cooking time** 55 minutes

Preheat the oven to 180°C (350°F). Lightly grease and line the base and side of a 23 cm (9 inch) spring-form cake tin with baking paper.

Melt the chocolate in a heatproof bowl set over a saucepan of simmering water, making sure the water doesn't touch the bowl. Cool. Sift together the flour, cocoa powder, bicarbonate of soda and salt, and set aside.

Use an electric mixer with a whisk attachment to whisk the eggs and sugar together on high until the mixture is thick and creamy. Pour the oil into the egg mix, followed by the cooled melted chocolate, and whisk to combine.

Fold one-third of the sifted ingredients through the chocolate mix followed by half of the yoghurt, repeat, then fold through the last of the dry ingredients, scraping the side of the bowl as you go.

Pour into the prepared tin. Bake for 35–40 minutes, or until a skewer inserted into the middle comes out clean. Leave to cool in the tin for 10 minutes, before turning out onto a wire rack to cool completely.

For the chocolate ganache: In a small saucepan, bring the cream to the boil, take off the heat, then add the chocolate and stir until melted, smooth and glossy. Allow to cool and thicken.

To assemble: Using a serrated knife, slice the cake into three even layers and spread each layer generously with raspberry jam and vanilla whipped cream. Top with the last layer of cake and pour over the softened chocolate ganache.

Notes: Chocolate ganache can be kept at room temperature for 2 days or stored in the fridge for up to 2 weeks. Before using, warm to soften in a heatproof bowl over a saucepan of simmering water, keeping the bowl clear of the water. The cake base can be made 2–3 days in advance and stored in an airtight container or can be frozen for up to 1 month. Defrost before using.

200 g (7 oz/1⅓ cups) chopped dark chocolate
185 g (6½ oz/1¼ cups) plain (all-purpose) flour
55 g (2 oz/½ cup) dark cocoa powder
½ teaspoon bicarbonate of soda (baking soda)
¼ teaspoon salt
4 eggs, at room temperature
295 g (10½ oz/1⅓ cups) caster (superfine) sugar
150 ml (5 fl oz) vegetable oil
260 g (9¼ oz/1 cup) plain yoghurt

CHOCOLATE GANACHE
100 ml (3½ fl oz) thin (pouring) cream
100 g (3½ oz/⅔ cup) chopped dark chocolate

320 g (11¼ oz/1 cup) Raspberry Jam (see page 226)
1 quantity Vanilla Whipped Cream (see page 221)

There is a cheesecake for just about everyone. Here, we use raspberries and white chocolate, but feel free to replace the raspberries with other berries or fresh fruit depending on the season.

BAKED WHITE CHOCOLATE RASPBERRY CHEESECAKES

Serves 10–12 • **Makes** one 23 cm round cake or eighteen 5 cm small cakes • **Preparation time** 30 minutes plus 1 hour refrigeration time • **Cooking time** 40 minutes for large cake; 15 minutes for small cakes

BISCUIT BASE

125 g (4½ oz) plain sweet biscuits, finely crushed

50 g (1¾ oz) butter, melted

TOPPING

500 g (1 lb 2 oz) cream cheese, at room temperature

2 eggs, at room temperature

220 g (7¾ oz/1 cup) caster (superfine) sugar

1 teaspoon natural vanilla extract

3 tablespoons cornflour (cornstarch)

400 g (14 oz) white chocolate, melted

300 ml (10½ fl oz) thickened (whipping) cream

125 g (4½ oz/1 cup) raspberries, fresh or frozen

Preheat the oven to 150°C (300°F). Lightly grease the base and side of a 23 cm (9 inch) spring-form cake tin or eighteen 5 cm (2 inch) mini cheesecake moulds.

Mix together the crushed biscuits and butter and press evenly into the base of the prepared tin/s. Set aside until ready to use.

In a food processor, process the cream cheese until smooth, add the eggs, sugar, vanilla and cornflour, and process until completely incorporated. Pulse in the melted chocolate and cream. Do not overmix.

Pour the filling over the crumb bases and scatter with raspberries.

For the single cake: Bake for 35–40 minutes.

For the mini cakes: Bake for 10–15 minutes.

The filling will not be completely set. Remove from the oven and allow to cool. Refrigerate until firm, about 1 hour. Remove from the tin/s to serve.

Note: You can store the cheesecake/s in the fridge for up to 5 days in an airtight container.

Your cake hopes and expectations will be answered with this tropically inspired cake. Packed with banana and pineapple, it will become the highlight of a summer get-together.

HUMMINGBIRD CAKE

Serves 8–10 • **Makes** one 23 cm round cake • **Preparation time** 1 hour • **Cooking time** 50 minutes

Preheat the oven to 180°C (350°F). Lightly grease and line the base and side of a 23 cm (9 inch) spring-form cake tin with baking paper.

Sift together the flour, cinnamon, bicarbonate of soda and salt, and set aside.

Use an electric mixer with a beater attachment to beat the eggs, sugar and vanilla until pale and creamy. Slowly add the oil and mix until combined. Mix in the pineapple with its juice and mashed bananas. Fold through the sifted dry ingredients.

Pour into the prepared tin. Bake for 45–50 minutes, or until a skewer inserted into the middle comes out clean. Leave to cool in the tin for 10 minutes, before turning out onto a wire rack to cool completely.

To assemble: Using a serrated knife, slice through the centre of the cake to form two even layers and cover the bottom layer with one-third of the cream cheese icing.

Place the other half of the cake on top and ice with the remaining icing. Alternatively, fill a piping (icing) bag fitted with a plain 1.5 cm (⅛ inch) nozzle with the remaining icing and pipe as desired, such as in the photograph opposite.

Peel the mangoes and slice cheeks very thinly to decorate the cake, loosely curving clusters of 2–3 slices.

Note: The cake base can be made 2–3 days in advance and stored in an airtight container or can be frozen for up to 1 month. Defrost before using.

450 g (1 lb/3 cups) plain (all-purpose) flour
1 teaspoon ground cinnamon
1 teaspoon bicarbonate of soda (baking soda)
1 teaspoon salt
3 eggs, at room temperature
385 g (13½ oz/1¾ cups) caster (superfine) sugar
1 teaspoon natural vanilla extract
310 ml (10¾ fl oz/1¼ cups) vegetable oil
250 g (9 oz) tinned crushed pineapple, with juice
4 ripe bananas, mashed

1 quantity Cream Cheese Icing (see page 26)
2 mangoes, ripe but firm

And so the debate goes on. Origin unproven, but there's one thing we all agree on — we love lamingtons! Ours have a layer of raspberry jam running through the middle. Best served with lashings of our vanilla whipped cream.

CHOCOLATE LAMINGTONS

300 g (10½ oz/2 cups) self-raising flour

40 g (1½ oz/⅓ cup) cornflour (cornstarch)

340 g (12 oz) butter, softened

330 g (11¾ oz/1½ cups) caster (superfine) sugar

1 teaspoon natural vanilla extract

6 eggs, at room temperature

100 ml (3½ fl oz) milk

LAMINGTON DIP

160 g (5¾ oz/1½ cups) dark cocoa powder

500 g (1 lb 2 oz/4 cups) icing (confectioners') sugar

100 g (3½ oz/⅔ cup) chopped dark chocolate

500 ml (17 fl oz/2 cups) boiling water

320 g (11¼ oz/1 cup) Raspberry Jam (see page 226)

350 g (12 oz/5⅓ cups) thread (shredded) coconut, for coating

1 quantity Vanilla Whipped Cream (see page 221), to serve

Makes 12 small cakes • **Preparation time** 45 minutes • **Cooking time** 30 minutes

Preheat the oven to 180°C (350°F). Lightly grease a 12-hole standard 250 ml (9 fl oz/1 cup) muffin tin.

Sift together the flour and cornflour, and set aside.

Use an electric mixer with a beater attachment to beat the butter and caster sugar until pale and creamy. Add the vanilla and then beat in the eggs one at a time. If the mix starts to curdle, add a tablespoon of the sifted flour. Fold in the rest of the sifted dry ingredients, then add the milk and mix until just incorporated.

Spoon the batter into the prepared tins. Bake for 25–30 minutes or until the sponge springs back when gently pressed on top. Cool in the tins before turning out.

For the lamington dip: Sift the cocoa powder and icing sugar into a medium bowl. Add the chopped dark chocolate and pour over the boiling water. Whisk until combined and the chocolate has melted. Strain through a sieve to remove any lumps and allow to cool.

To assemble: Cut each sponge in half and sandwich together with the raspberry jam. Carefully dip each one into the lamington dip, drain off any excess chocolate and roll in the coconut threads to coat. Place on a wire rack to dry.

Serve with vanilla whipped cream.

Note: Store in an airtight container for up to 2–3 days.

And just in case you don't have a carrot cake recipe, here's ours. Carrot cake has been a staple in our repertoire for many, many years.

A great sales pitch from one of our staff: 'It is moist, packed with flavour and healthy, right?! Carrots are a vegetable after all.'

CARROT AND WALNUT LOAF

Serves 10–12 • **Makes** one 23 cm round cake or two 10 x 20 cm loaves • **Preparation time** 1 hour 20 minutes • **Cooking time** 1 hour

Preheat the oven to 180°C (350°F). Lightly grease and line the base and sides of a 23 cm (9 inch) spring-form cake tin, or two 10 x 20 cm (4 x 8 inch) loaf (bar) tins, with baking paper.

Sift together the flour, mixed spice, baking powder, bicarbonate of soda and salt, and set aside.

In a second bowl, use an electric mixer with a beater attachment to beat the eggs, caster sugar and oil until frothy.

In another large bowl combine the grated carrot, walnuts and pineapple. Mix in the egg, sugar and oil mixture. Mix thoroughly then fold in all the sifted dry ingredients.

Pour into the prepared tin/s. Bake for 45–50 minutes, or until a skewer inserted into the middle of the cake or loaves comes out clean. Leave to cool in the tin/s for 10 minutes, before turning out onto a wire rack to cool completely.

For the cream cheese icing: Use an electric mixer with a beater attachment to beat the butter and icing sugar until pale and creamy. Gradually add the cream cheese bit by bit. Keep beating until all the cream cheese is combined and thoroughly mixed.

For the seed praline: Spread the seeds on a baking tray lined with baking paper. In a medium saucepan, combine 2 tablespoons (1¼ fl oz/40 ml) water and the sugar. Bring to the boil, without stirring, over medium heat until the sugar dissolves. Keep on cooking until golden amber in colour. Quickly pour the toffee over the seeds to coat. Allow to set and cool, then break into shards.

Ice the cake or loaves generously with cream cheese icing and decorate with shards of seed praline.

Notes: The cake base can be made 2–3 days in advance and stored in an airtight container or frozen for up to 1 month. Defrost before using. Cream cheese icing will keep in the fridge for a week. The praline can be stored, in pieces, in an airtight container for up to 2 weeks.

375 g (13 oz/2½ cups) plain (all-purpose) flour

3 teaspoons mixed spice

2 teaspoons baking powder

1½ teaspoons bicarbonate of soda (baking soda)

1½ teaspoons salt

4 eggs, at room temperature

330 g (11¾ oz/1½ cups) caster (superfine) sugar

375 ml (13 fl oz/1½ cups) vegetable oil

400 g (14 oz/2½ cups) grated carrot

140 g (5 oz/1 cup) walnut pieces, toasted and roughly chopped

150 g (5½ oz) tinned crushed pineapple, drained

CREAM CHEESE ICING

125 g (4½ oz/½ cup) unsalted butter, softened

125 g (4½ oz/1 cup) icing (confectioners') sugar, sifted

500 g (1 lb 2 oz) cream cheese, softened

SEED PRALINE

145 g (5 oz/1 cup) mixed seeds (sesame, sunflower, pepitas, pumpkin seeds)

220 g (7¾ oz/1 cup) caster (superfine) sugar

THE COOK AND BAKER

Not only are these cakes incredibly more-ish and moist, they are also gluten- and dairy-free, making them the perfect all-rounder.

FLOURLESS MANDARIN MARMALADE CAKES

MANDARIN PURÉE

500 g (1 lb 2 oz) mandarins

5 eggs, at room temperature
220 g (7¾ oz/1 cup) caster (superfine) sugar
250 g (9 oz/2½ cups) almond meal
1 teaspoon baking powder
flaked almonds, to scatter

320 g (11¼ oz/1 cup) Mandarin Marmalade (see page 225)

icing (confectioners') sugar, for dusting

Serves 12 • **Makes** one 23 cm round cake or 12 standard muffins • **Preparation time** 25 minutes • **Cooking time** 1 hour 30 minutes for cake; 1 hour 10 minutes for muffins

For the mandarin purée: Place the mandarins in a medium saucepan, cover with water and bring to the boil. Reduce heat to medium and cook until the mandarin peel is soft, about 45 minutes.

Remove from the water, allow to cool, then cut open, remove the seeds and chop the mandarins roughly. Purée until smooth. You will need 300 g (10½ oz/1⅓ cups) of mandarin purée.

Preheat the oven to 180°C (350°F). Lightly grease and line the base and side of a 23 cm (9 inch) spring-form cake tin with baking paper or a 12-hole 80 ml (2½ fl oz/⅓ cup) muffin tin with paper cases.

Use an electric mixer with a whisk attachment to whisk the eggs and sugar together until combined. Do not overbeat the eggs as this will aerate the mixture. Add the mandarin purée, almond meal and baking powder and mix well.

Pour into the prepared tin/s, scatter over the flaked almonds, and spread the marmalade over the cake/s.

For the single cake: Bake for 40–45 minutes.

For the muffins: Bake for 20–25 minutes.

The cakes/muffins are ready when they spring back when pressed, or when a skewer inserted into the middle comes out clean.

Leave to cool completely before removing from the tin/s. Dust with icing sugar before serving.

Notes: The mandarin marmalade and purée can be made well in advance, making these cakes very quick to throw together. Left-over purée can be stored in the fridge for up to 1 week in an airtight container or can be frozen for up to 1 month.

The cake/s can be made 2–3 days in advance and stored in an airtight container or can be frozen for up to 1 month. Defrost before using.

Our 'Southern Belle' is a light chocolate cake layered and covered with vanilla frosting. It gets its deep red colour from — dare we say it — red food colouring. As an alternative to vanilla frosting you can use cream cheese icing. For an impressive result, finish the cake with a dusting of fine red velvet cake crumbs, as shown in the photograph opposite.

RED VELVET CAKE

Serves 10–12 • **Makes** one 23 cm round cake • **Preparation time** 1 hour • **Cooking time** 1 hour 10 minutes

Preheat the oven to 180°C (350°F). Lightly grease and line the base and side of a 23 cm (9 inch) spring-form cake tin with baking paper.

In a large bowl, sift together the flour, cocoa powder, bicarbonate of soda and salt, and set aside.

Use an electric mixer with a whisk attachment to whisk together the oil, buttermilk, sugar, eggs, food colouring, vinegar and vanilla. Gently mix through the sifted dry ingredients until well incorporated. Do not overmix as this develops gluten, which leads to a tough cake.

Pour into the prepared tin. Bake for 50–60 minutes, or until a skewer inserted into the middle of the cake comes out clean. Leave to cool in the tin for 10 minutes, before turning out onto a wire rack to cool completely.

For the vanilla frosting: In a medium saucepan, whisk the flour and milk together until smooth. Place over medium heat and continue to whisk until the milk and flour thickens to a paste-like consistency. Let it cool, stirring occasionally.

Add the sugar, vanilla and salt and transfer to the bowl of an electric mixer fitted with a paddle attachment. Beat in the butter, a little at a time until it is fully incorporated. The mixture will look split but keep beating on high until the icing becomes homogenous.

To assemble: Using a serrated knife, slice the cake into three even layers. Spread the bottom two layers with raspberry jam and vanilla frosting. Top with the last layer and ice with the remaining frosting, covering the sides as well. Cover with a dusting of red velvet cake crumbs, if using.

Notes: The cake base can be made 2–3 days in advance and stored in an airtight container or frozen for up to 1 month. Defrost before using. The vanilla frosting will keep in the fridge for up to 1 week.

335 g (11¾ oz/2¼ cups) plain (all-purpose) flour
1 tablespoon cocoa powder
1 teaspoon bicarbonate of soda (baking soda)
1 teaspoon salt
185 ml (6 fl oz/¾ cup) vegetable oil
345 ml (12 fl oz/1½ cups) buttermilk
295 g (10½ oz/1⅓ cups) caster (superfine) sugar
2 eggs, at room temperature
1 tablespoon red food colouring
1 teaspoon white wine vinegar
1 teaspoon natural vanilla extract
320 g (11¼ oz/1 cup) Raspberry Jam (see page 226)
Red Velvet Cake crumbs (optional)

VANILLA FROSTING

75 g (2¾ oz/½ cup) plain (all-purpose) flour
480 ml (17 fl oz) milk
385 g (13½ oz/1¾ cups) caster (superfine) sugar
1 tablespoon natural vanilla extract
¼ teaspoon salt
450 g (1 lb) unsalted butter, softened

We always thought there were too many muffins in this world so we resisted making them. But after many requests, we gave in.

These gluten-free muffins provide the ultimate excuse for having chocolate for breakfast.

FLOURLESS CHOCOLATE RASPBERRY MUFFINS

softened butter, for greasing

cocoa powder, for dusting

320 g (11¼ oz) unsalted butter, chopped

400 g (14 oz/2⅔ cups) dark chocolate, chopped

10 eggs, at room temperature, separated

330 g (11¾ oz/1½ cups) caster (superfine) sugar

325 g (11½ oz/3¼ cups) almond meal

500 g (1 lb 2 oz/2 cups) fresh raspberries

Makes 15–16 muffins • **Preparation time** 25 minutes • **Cooking time** 35 minutes

Preheat the oven to 180°C (350°F). Lightly grease fifteen to sixteen 250 ml (9 fl oz/1 cup) dariole moulds with softened butter and dust with cocoa powder, or place 16 paper cases into standard 250 ml (9 fl oz/1 cup) muffin tins.

In a medium saucepan, melt the butter over low heat, then add the chocolate and stir until melted. Keep warm.

Use an electric mixer with a whisk attachment to whisk the egg whites. Whisk until stiff (but not dry) peaks form. Sprinkle 110 g (3¾ oz/ ½ cup) of the caster sugar over the egg whites and fold in. Set aside.

Mix the almond meal, egg yolks and remaining caster sugar into the butter and chocolate mixture. Then gently fold through the egg whites.

Spoon the mixture evenly between the moulds, filling to three-quarters, then place 3–4 raspberries on top of each. Bake for 25–30 minutes until risen and firm. Leave to cool in the moulds before turning out.

Notes: These muffins will keep for 2–3 days in an airtight container. They can also be frozen for up to 1 month. Defrost before serving.

Impressive and dramatic to say the least! The aromatic spices and caramelised roasted pears make this a comforting cake for the cooler months. This recipe is a bit more involved than most of the others but well worth the effort.

SPICED GINGER AND ROASTED PEAR CAKE

Serves 10–12 • **Makes** one 23 cm round cake • **Preparation time** 45 minutes • **Cooking time** 1 hour 50 minutes

Preheat the oven to 160°C (315°F). Lightly grease and line the base and side of a 23 cm (9 inch) spring-form cake tin with baking paper.

In a large bowl, sift together the flour, ginger, cinnamon, bicarbonate of soda and salt.

In a medium bowl, whisk together the eggs, caster sugar, golden syrup, hot water and oil. Pour onto the dry ingredients and stir until combined. Do not overmix.

Pour into the lined cake tin. Bake for 70–80 minutes, or until a skewer inserted into the middle comes out clean. Leave to cool in the tin for 10 minutes, before turning out onto a wire rack to cool completely.

For the roasted pears: Halve the pears, remove the cores and cut each half into 4 wedges. Toss with the brown sugar and cinnamon. Line a baking tray with baking paper, spread over the pear pieces and roast in the oven at 180°C (350°F) for 25–30 minutes. Let cool. These can be cooked in advance and used as needed.

To assemble: Using a serrated knife, slice through the centre of the cake to form two even layers and spread the bottom layer with one-third of the cream cheese icing. Place the other half of the cake on top and ice with the remaining icing. Top with the roasted pears and walnut praline, if using.

Notes: The cake base can be made 2–3 days in advance and stored in an airtight container or can be frozen for up to 1 month. Defrost before using.

485 g (1 lb 1 oz/3¼ cups) plain (all-purpose) flour
3 teaspoons ground ginger
1½ teaspoons ground cinnamon
1½ teaspoons bicarbonate of soda (baking soda)
¾ teaspoon salt
2 eggs, at room temperature, lightly whisked
220 g (7¾ oz/1 cup) caster (superfine) sugar
260 g (9¼ oz/¾ cup) golden syrup (light treacle)
250 ml (9 fl oz/1 cup) hot water
250 ml (9 fl oz/1 cup) vegetable oil

ROASTED PEARS
4 firm ripe pears
245 g (8¾ oz/1⅓ cups, lightly packed) light brown sugar
½ teaspoon ground cinnamon

1 quantity Cream Cheese Icing (see page 26)
1 quantity Walnut Praline (optional) (see page 102)

A godsend for the gluten- and nut-intolerant folks out there. Our recipe is baked in two stages, which creates a dense base with a light, fudge-like topping. Piled high with berries and served with our vanilla whipped cream or some crème fraîche, it is a little slice of heaven. Total decadence!

FLOURLESS CHOCOLATE FUDGE CAKE

240 g (8½ oz) unsalted butter, chopped

360 g (12¾ oz) dark chocolate, chopped

285 g (10 oz/1½ cups, lightly packed) light brown sugar

5 eggs, at room temperature, separated

cocoa powder, for dusting

Serves 10–12 • **Makes** one 23 cm round cake • **Preparation time** 30 minutes plus cooling time • **Cooking time** 1 hour 15 minutes

Preheat the oven to 180°C (350°F). Lightly grease and line the base and side of a 23 cm (9 inch) spring-form cake tin with baking paper.

In a medium saucepan, melt the butter over low heat then take off the heat, add the chocolate and stir until melted.

In a small saucepan, mix together the sugar and 60 ml (2 fl oz/¼ cup) water. Bring to the boil over medium–high heat. Pour the hot syrup over the melted butter and chocolate and stir until combined. Stir in the egg yolks, then pour into a medium bowl and set aside.

Use an electric mixer with a whisk attachment to whisk the egg whites until stiff, but not dry, peaks form. Using a rubber spatula, gently fold the beaten egg whites into the chocolate mixture until combined, making sure there are no streaks of egg white.

Pour half of the mixture into the prepared tin, gently spread level. Bake for 30 minutes, or until a skewer inserted into the middle comes out almost clean. Remove from the oven and let cool completely.

Flatten the top of the cake, pour over the remaining batter then return to the oven and bake for another 25–30 minutes. Leave to cool completely before removing from the tin. Dust with cocoa powder and serve.

Notes: The cake can be made 2–3 days in advance. Keep covered in an airtight container in the fridge. Serve at room temperature.

These muffins are wholesome, and full of fibre and good-for-me ingredients. And the riper the bananas, the sweeter the muffins. The sour cream adds a tangy depth to the flavour and extra moistness. Light and satisfying.

MORNING GLORY MUFFIN

Makes 12 muffins • **Preparation time** 20 minutes plus 30 minutes soaking time for raisins and bran mixture • **Cooking time** 40 minutes

Preheat the oven to 170°C (325°F). Lightly grease and line a 12-hole standard 250 ml (9 fl oz/1 cup) muffin tin with paper cases.

In a small bowl, cover the raisins with hot water and set aside for 30 minutes to plump up.

In a medium bowl mix the bran flakes, milk, sour cream, eggs and banana until well combined. Let stand for 25–30 minutes.

In another bowl, mix together the millet, linseed and sunflower seeds, and set these aside.

Add the brown sugar and molasses to the bran mixture and stir until well combined. Drain the raisins, add to the bran mixture, and stir.

Sift together the flour, baking powder, bicarbonate of soda and salt. Gently fold into the wet ingredients until just combined. Spoon into the prepared tins, filling to the rim. Sprinkle over the seed mix.

Bake for 35–40 minutes until golden brown and the muffins spring back when pressed in the middle. Cool in the tin before turning out.

Note: These muffins keep for 1–2 days in an airtight container.

170 g (6 oz/1 cup) raisins

200 g (7 oz/2⅔ cups) bran flakes

300 ml (10½ fl oz) milk

420 g (14¾ oz) sour cream

2 eggs, lightly beaten

2 ripe bananas, mashed

50 g (1¾ oz/¼ cup) hulled millet

40 g (1½ oz/¼ cup) linseeds (flaxseeds)

30 g (1 oz/¼ cup) sunflower seeds

100 g (3½ oz/½ cup, lightly packed) light brown sugar

2 tablespoons molasses

335 g (11¾ oz/2½ cups) plain (all-purpose) flour

2 teaspoons baking powder

1 teaspoon bicarbonate of soda (baking soda)

1 teaspoon salt

This cake reminds Cherie of her years living and cooking in the Cook Islands. Full of coconut flavour, tangy passionfruit and embellished with even more coconut, it is the go-to recipe for all coconut lovers.

COCONUT AND PASSIONFRUIT CURD CAKE

300 g (10½ oz) butter, softened

550 g (1 lb 4 oz/2½ cups) caster (superfine) sugar

finely grated zest of 2 lemons

7 eggs, at room temperature

450 g (1 lb/3 cups) plain (all-purpose) flour

2½ teaspoons baking powder

195 g (6¾ oz/3 cups) thread (shredded) coconut

180 g (6½ oz/2 cups) desiccated coconut

200 g (7 oz) plain yoghurt

1 quantity Cream Cheese Icing (see page 26)

185 g (6½ oz/¾ cup) Passionfruit Curd (see page 228)

120 g (4¼ oz) coconut flakes

Serves 10–12 • **Makes** one 23 cm round cake • **Preparation time** 40 minutes • **Cooking time** 1 hour

Preheat the oven to 180°C (350°F). Lightly grease and line the base and side of a 23 cm (9 inch) spring-form cake tin with baking paper.

Use an electric mixer with a beater attachment to beat the butter, sugar and lemon zest until pale and creamy. Add the eggs one at a time, mixing well after each addition. Sift the flour and baking powder, and mix with the creamed ingredients until just combined. Fold through the thread and desiccated coconuts and the yoghurt.

Pour into the prepared tin. Bake for 55–60 minutes, or until a skewer inserted into the middle of the cake comes out clean. Leave to cool in the tin for 10 minutes, before turning out onto a wire rack to cool completely.

To assemble: Using a serrated knife, slice through the centre of the cake to form two even layers. Spread the bottom layer with one-third of the cream cheese icing and all the passionfruit curd. Place the other half of the cake on top and ice with the remaining icing, covering the sides as well. Coat with the coconut flakes.

Notes: The cake base can be made 2–3 days in advance and stored in an airtight container or can be frozen for up to 1 month. Defrost before using.

Nothing says celebration like a layered cake. Once iced with vanilla buttercream, it is a great blank canvas to let your imagination run wild. We like to decorate with an array of seasonal flowers.

Don't be alarmed by the number of egg yolks — this is what gives the cake character and its lovely yellow colour.

BUTTER CAKE

Serves 10–12 • **Makes** one 23 cm round cake • **Preparation time** 1 hour 25 minutes • **Cooking time** 1 hour 15 minutes

Preheat the oven to 160°C (315°F). Lightly grease and line the base and side of a 23 cm (9 inch) spring-form cake tin with baking paper.

In a bowl, sift together the flour, baking powder and salt, and set aside. In a separate bowl, combine the buttermilk and vanilla. Use a stand mixer to beat the butter and sugar until pale and creamy. Beat in the egg yolks in three additions.

Mix in one-third of the sifted flour and half the buttermilk, repeat, finishing with the flour. Beat until just combined each time. Pour into the prepared tin and bake for 55–60 minutes, or until a skewer inserted into the middle comes out clean. Leave in the tin for 10 minutes, before turning out onto a wire rack to cool completely.

For the buttercream: In a small saucepan over medium heat, combine the sugar with 100 ml (3½ fl oz) water. Bring slowly to the boil and cook for 5–10 minutes, until it reaches 120°C (235°F) on a sugar thermometer, making sure to keep an eye on it, then remove from the heat.

Meanwhile, combine the egg whites and cream of tartar using an electric mixer fitted with a whisk attachment. Whisk the egg whites until soft peaks form. On low speed, carefully pour in the sugar syrup down the side of the bowl so that the hot syrup doesn't splatter. Increase the speed to high and beat for 5–10 minutes, until the mixture has cooled. Reduce to medium, and add the butter a little at a time. If the icing curdles, increase the speed to high and slowly keep adding the butter until it is smooth and thick. Stir in the vanilla.

To assemble: Use a serrated knife to slice the cake into three even layers. Spread the bottom two layers with raspberry jam and half the buttercream. Place the last layer on top and completely cover with buttercream.

Notes: The cake base will keep for 2–3 days in an airtight container or frozen for up to 1 month. Defrost before using. The egg whites can be frozen and used to make the Pavlova Wreath (see page 136) or Meringue (see page 62).

320 g (11¼ oz) plain (all-purpose) flour
2½ teaspoons baking powder
½ teaspoon salt
250 ml (9 fl oz/1 cup) buttermilk
1 teaspoon natural vanilla extract
280 g (10 oz) butter, softened
295 g (10½ oz/1⅓ cups) caster (superfine) sugar
14 egg yolks, at room temperature

VANILLA BUTTERCREAM
440 g (15½ oz/2 cups) caster (superfine) sugar
5 egg whites, at room temperature
1 teaspoon cream of tartar
700 g (1 lb 9 oz) butter, diced and softened
1 tablespoon natural vanilla extract

320 g (11¼ oz/1 cup) Raspberry Jam (see page 226)

We celebrated our first harvest of honey from our rooftop hives by baking this cake. This cake is all about the honey. The fragrance wafting from the oven when it's baking is intoxicating.

Thanks to Queen Latifah and her hard-working bees!

QUEEN LATIFAH'S HONEY SPICE CAKE

150 g (5½ oz/1 cup) plain (all-purpose) flour
½ teaspoon baking powder
½ teaspoon ground cinnamon
½ teaspoon ground allspice
125 g (4½ oz) honey
50 g (1¾ oz) golden syrup (light treacle)
140 g (5 oz) butter, chopped
45 g (1½ oz/¼ cup, lightly packed) light brown sugar
2 eggs, at room temperature
1 tablespoon finely grated ginger

Serves 10 • **Makes** one 10 x 20 cm loaf • **Preparation time** 20 minutes • **Cooking time** 1 hour 5 minutes

Preheat the oven to 160°C (315°F). Lightly grease a 10 x 20 cm (4 x 8 inch) loaf (bar) tin. Line the base and sides with baking paper extending over the two long sides.

In a bowl, sift together the flour, baking powder, cinnamon and allspice, and set aside.

In a small saucepan, over low heat, gently warm the honey, golden syrup, butter and sugar until the butter is just melted.

Transfer the honey mixture to the bowl of an electric mixer fitted with a whisk attachment and beat for 2–3 minutes at medium speed. Add the eggs and grated ginger and continue beating until well combined. Fold in the sifted dry ingredients.

Pour into the prepared tin and bake for 50–60 minutes, until golden brown or until a skewer inserted into the middle of the loaf comes out clean. Leave to cool in the tin for 10 minutes, before turning out onto a wire rack to cool completely. Cut into thick slices to serve.

Notes: The cake can be made 2–3 days in advance and stored in an airtight container or can be frozen for up to 1 month. Defrost before using.

CHAPTER № 2

SWEET TARTS

With busy schedules and time constraints,
the art of making tarts is disappearing
from the home cook's repertoire.
These are not complicated tarts, but
ones to be celebrated and revisited.
Our recipes are easy and infallible.

Our take on Strawberries and Cream, these are best made as individual tarts as it does not cut well as one large tart. You can substitute the strawberries for any seasonal fruit.

STRAWBERRY AND VANILLA CUSTARD TARTS

Makes eight 10 cm tarts • **Preparation time** 30 minutes plus 30 minutes freezing time for pastry and 1 hour refrigeration time for pastry crème • **Cooking time** 30 minutes

Preheat the oven to 180°C (350°F). Lightly grease eight 10 cm (4 inch) round loose-based fluted flan (tart) tins.

On a lightly floured surface, roll out the pastry to 3 mm (⅛ inch) thick. Line the tins and trim any excess pastry. Cover with plastic wrap and rest in the freezer for at least 30 minutes.

To blind bake the tart cases, line the tins with pieces of crumpled baking paper and pour in some baking beads or uncooked rice or dried beans. Bake for 10–15 minutes. Remove the paper and weights, return to the oven and bake until golden, approximately a further 10–15 minutes. Remove from the oven and allow to cool.

Put the pastry crème in the bowl of an electric mixer fitted with a paddle attachment. Mix on low speed until smooth.

Using electric beaters, whip the cream to a soft peak. Fold this whipped cream through the pastry crème mixture and chill in the fridge for about 1 hour.

Spoon or pipe the custard filling into each tart shell, top with a dollop of jam and some strawberries. Serve immediately. These tarts are best eaten within 2–3 hours once filled.

Notes: You can bake the pastry cases in advance and store in an airtight container for up to 1 week. The pastry crème can also be made and refrigerated up to 3–4 days ahead.

1 quantity Sweet Pastry (see page 218)
1 quantity Vanilla Pastry Crème
 (see page 222)

200 ml (7 fl oz) thin (pouring) cream
165 g (5¾ oz/½ cup) Raspberry Jam
 (see page 226), to dollop
500 g (1 lb 2 oz/3⅓ cups) strawberries,
 hulled, then sliced or quartered

We created this tart after the cult following for our plum tart, when the plum season ended and we had customers suffering from withdrawals. You can also use granny smith apples and glaze with melted honey, if you prefer. Great served piping hot from the oven with generous amounts of ice cream.

PEAR AND ALMOND TART

300 g (10½ oz/2 cups) plain
(all-purpose) flour
150 g (5½ oz) cold butter, diced
250 g (9 oz) caster (superfine) sugar
pinch of salt
2 egg yolks, at room temperature
1 teaspoon natural vanilla extract
185 g (6½ oz/¾ cup) Frangipane
(see page 54)
4 firm ripe pears
3 tablespoons light brown sugar
½ teaspoon ground cinnamon
4 tablespoons apricot jam, to glaze

Serves 8–10 • **Makes** one 20 x 30 cm tart • **Preparation time** 40 minutes plus 30 minutes chilling time for pastry • **Cooking time** 55 minutes

Preheat the oven to 180°C (350°F). Lightly grease and line a 20 x 30 cm (8 x 12 inch) slab tin with baking paper, ensuring the sides of the tin are fully lined.

Put the flour and butter into a food processor and process until the mixture resembles breadcrumbs. Add the sugar and salt, and mix again. Add the egg yolks, 2 tablespoons cold water and the vanilla and bring together until the mixture forms a ball.

Press the pastry evenly into the prepared tin and chill in the fridge for 30 minutes. Remove from the fridge and spread over the frangipane.

Halve and core the pears. Using a mandolin or sharp knife, slice the pears thinly and scatter the slices on top of the frangipane. Sprinkle with the combined brown sugar and cinnamon. Bake for 45–50 minutes until cooked and golden brown.

Transfer to a wire rack and allow to cool in the tin. Gently heat the apricot jam in a small saucepan, then pour through a sieve into a bowl. Brush the pears liberally with the glaze. Cut evenly into 8–10 pieces. Serve warm or at room temperature.

Note: This tart can be stored in the fridge for up to 3–4 days.

The frangipane in these tarts pairs beautifully with figs, stonefruit, poached pears or slow-cooked quince. In summer our favourite fruit to use is peaches or nectarines.

ROASTED PEACH AND ALMOND TARTS

Makes eight 10 cm tarts • **Preparation time** 50 minutes plus 30 minutes freezing time for pastry • **Cooking time** 1 hour 20 minutes

For the frangipane: In the bowl of an electric mixer fitted with a paddle attachment, beat together the butter, sugar and vanilla on a medium speed until pale and creamy.

Add the eggs, one at a time, making sure each is well combined before adding the next egg. Add the almond meal, flour and salt. Beat until thoroughly incorporated.

Preheat the oven to 180°C (350°F). Lightly grease eight 10 cm (4 inch) round loose-based flan fluted (tart) tins.

On a lightly floured surface, roll out the pastry to 3 mm (⅛ inch) thick. Line the tins and trim any excess pastry. Cover with plastic wrap and rest in the freezer for at least 30 minutes.

To blind bake the tart cases, line the tins with pieces of crumpled baking paper and pour in some baking beads or uncooked rice or dried beans. Bake for 10–15 minutes. Remove the paper and weights, return to the oven and bake until golden, approximately a further 10–15 minutes. Remove from the oven and allow to cool.

For the roasted peaches: Cut the peaches in half, remove the stones, then cut in half again. Toss with sugar, place on a baking tray lined with baking paper, then bake for 25 minutes or until just soft. Leave to cool.

Three-quarters fill each tart case with the frangipane. Place 2 pieces of peach on top and lightly press them into the frangipane, then bake for 20–25 minutes or until the frangipane is firm. Test by inserting a skewer – it should come out clean.

Finish off with 2 more pieces of peach, a spoonful of crème fraîche and almonds, and dust with icing sugar. These tarts are best eaten on the day they are made. Serve hot or at room temperature.

Notes: Pastry cases can be made in advance and stored in an airtight container for up to 1 week. Frangipane can be stored covered and refrigerated for up to 1 week, or frozen in a sealed container for up to 1 month. Make sure to bring it back to room temperature before using.

FRANGIPANE (ALMOND CREAM)
Makes 900 g (2 lb)
220 g (7¾ oz) butter, softened
220 g (7¾ oz/1 cup) caster
    (superfine) sugar
½ teaspoon natural vanilla extract
4 eggs, at room temperature
200 g (7 oz/2 cups) almond meal
50 g (1¾ oz/⅓ cup) plain (all-purpose)
    flour
½ teaspoon salt

1 quantity Sweet Pastry (see page 218)

ROASTED PEACHES
6–8 ripe peaches
110 g (3¾ oz/½ cup) caster (superfine)
    sugar

crème fraîche or thick cream, to serve
50 g (1¾ oz/½ cup) flaked almonds,
    lightly toasted, to serve
icing (confectioners') sugar, to dust

A weekend special, this tart draws our customers from far and wide. The crispy pastry crust makes a perfect case for the creamy, velvety custard. A nostalgic memory for many, these don't disappoint!

BAKED CUSTARD TART

1 quantity Sweet Pastry (see page 218)

2 vanilla beans
600 ml (21 fl oz) thin (pouring) cream
100 ml (3½ fl oz) milk
10 egg yolks, at room temperature
75 g (2¾ oz/⅓ cup) caster (superfine) sugar

freshly grated nutmeg, to dust

Serves 8–10 • **Makes** one 23 cm tart • **Preparation time** 25 minutes plus 30 minutes chilling time for pastry • **Cooking time** 1 hour 30 minutes

Preheat the oven to 180°C (350°F). Lightly grease a round 23 cm (9 inch) loose-based fluted flan (tart) tin.

On a lightly floured surface, roll out the pastry to 3 mm (⅛ inch) thick. Line the tin and trim off any excess pastry. Cover with plastic wrap and refrigerate for 30 minutes.

To blind bake the tart case, line the tin with a piece of crumpled baking paper and pour in some baking beads or uncooked rice or dried beans. Bake for 15 minutes. Remove the paper and weights, return to the oven and bake until golden, approximately a further 15 minutes. Remove from the oven and allow to cool. Reduce the oven temperature to 140°C (275°F).

Split the vanilla beans in half lengthways, scrape the seeds from the pods with the tip of a sharp knife, and set aside.

In a large bowl, whisk the cream, milk, egg yolks, caster sugar and vanilla seeds until combined. Strain through a fine-mesh sieve and skim off any froth from the surface.

Pour into the tart shell. Bake for 50–60 minutes or until just set, then dust with nutmeg. Transfer to a wire rack and allow to cool in the tin. Slice into wedges to serve.

Serve at room temperature. This tart is best eaten the day it is baked.

Note: You can bake the pastry case in advance and store in an airtight container for up to 1 week.

This has to be one of our most asked for recipes, and after long deliberation we have decided to share this recipe with you.

The beautiful crimson colour of ripe plums makes this tart irresistible. Blood plums are our favourite to use when available, but most importantly the fruit should always be at its peak of ripeness.

PLUM TART

Serves 8–10 • **Makes** one 20 x 30 cm tart • **Preparation time** 35 minutes plus 30 minutes chilling time for pastry • **Cooking time** 55 minutes

Preheat the oven to 180°C (350°F). Lightly grease and line a 20 x 30 cm (8 x 12 inch) slab tin with baking paper, ensuring that the sides of the tin are fully lined.

Put the flour and butter into a food processor and process until the mixture resembles breadcrumbs. Add the sugar and salt and mix again. Mix in the egg yolks, 2 tablespoons cold water and the vanilla and bring together until the ingredients form a ball.

Quarter the plums and remove the stones.

Press the pastry evenly into the prepared tin, place the plums on top in rows, sprinkle with the extra sugar and bake for 45–50 minutes until cooked and golden.

Transfer to a wire rack and allow to cool in the tin. Gently heat the apricot jam in a small saucepan, then pour through a sieve into a bowl. Brush the plums liberally with the glaze. Cut evenly into 8–10 pieces. Serve warm or at room temperature.

Note: This tart can be stored in the fridge for up to 3–4 days.

300 g (10½ oz/2 cups) plain (all-purpose) flour
150 g (5½ oz) cold butter, diced
250 g (9 oz) caster (superfine) sugar, plus 3 tablespoons for sprinkling
pinch of salt
2 egg yolks, at room temperature
1 teaspoon natural vanilla extract
750 g (1 lb 10 oz) firm ripe plums

4 tablespoons apricot jam, to glaze

The tartness of the apricots cuts through the richness of the dark chocolate. We serve this simply with a dollop of crème fraîche or thickened cream. This tart is amazing!

DARK CHOCOLATE APRICOT TART

1 quantity Sweet Pastry (see page 218)

APRICOT PASTE

200 g (7 oz/1¼ cups) dried apricots, finely chopped

2 tablespoons lemon juice

CHOCOLATE FILLING

150 ml (5 fl oz) thin (pouring) cream

150 g (5½ oz) butter, chopped

450 g (1 lb/3 cups) chopped dark chocolate

5 egg yolks, at room temperature

2 whole eggs, at room temperature

150 g (5½ oz/⅔ cup) caster (superfine) sugar

crème fraîche or thick cream, to serve

Serves 8–10 • **Makes** one 23 cm tart • **Preparation time** 40 minutes plus 30 minutes chilling time for pastry • **Cooking time** 1 hour

Preheat the oven to 180°C (350°F). Lightly grease a round 23 cm (9 inch) loose-based fluted flan (tart) tin.

On a lightly floured surface, roll out the pastry to 3 mm (⅛ inch) thick. Line the tin and trim any excess pastry. Cover with plastic wrap and refrigerate for 30 minutes.

To blind bake the tart case, line the tin with a piece of crumpled baking paper and pour in some baking beads or uncooked rice or dried beans. Bake for 15 minutes. Remove the paper and weights, return to the oven and bake until golden, approximately a further 15 minutes. Remove from the oven and allow to cool.

To make the paste, cook the apricots with 4 tablespoons water and the lemon juice in a small saucepan over low heat. Simmer for 5 minutes or until soft. Purée in a blender until smooth; this purée should be slightly sharp. Let cool and then spread onto the base of the blind-baked tart shell.

To make the chocolate filling bring the cream and butter to the boil in a medium saucepan over medium–low heat. Take off the heat and add the chocolate, then stir until melted and smooth. Let cool a little.

In the bowl of an electric mixer, fitted with a whisk attachment, put the egg yolks, whole eggs and caster sugar. Whisk until pale and creamy, then fold the chocolate mixture into the beaten eggs, and stir until all incorporated.

Pour the chocolate filling into the tart case over the apricot purée. Bake for approximately 8–10 minutes. Transfer to a wire rack and allow to cool in the tin. The filling should still be wobbly, with a slight crust formed on top. This will firm up once the tart has cooled.

Cut into wedges and serve with crème fraîche or thick cream. This tart is best eaten on the day it is baked.

Note: The baked pastry case can be stored in an airtight container for up to 1 week. The apricot paste will keep, covered, for up to 1 week in the fridge.

We love these tarts. The size makes them absolutely guilt free and we defy you to stop at just one. A perfect combination of crispy pastry, tangy passionfruit and velvety meringue.

PASSIONFRUIT MERINGUE TARTS

Makes 24 mini tarts • **Preparation time** 50 minutes plus 30 minutes freezing time for pastry • **Cooking time** 40 minutes

Preheat the oven to 180°C (350°F). Lightly grease a 24-hole 4 cm (1½ inch) mini muffin tin.

On a lightly floured surface, roll out the pastry to 3 mm (⅛ inch) thick. Cut circles with a 7 cm (2¾ inch) plain pastry cutter and line the tins. Cover with plastic wrap and rest in the freezer for at least 30 minutes.

To blind bake the tart cases, line the tins with small pieces of crumpled baking paper and pour in some baking beads or uncooked rice or dried beans. Bake for 10 minutes. Remove the paper and weights, return to the oven and bake until golden, approximately a further 10 minutes. Remove from the oven and allow to cool.

For the passionfruit filling: In a medium bowl, whisk the condensed milk, lemon juice, sieved passionfruit pulp and egg yolks until combined. Strain into a pouring jug, then pour the filling into the blind-baked tart cases. Bake for 5–8 minutes or until just set.

For the meringue: Put the sugar into a small saucepan with 60 ml (2 fl oz/¼ cup) water and the pinch of cream of tartar. Bring to the boil and cook to the soft ball stage (118°C/244°F) on a sugar thermometer.

Put the egg whites and vanilla into the bowl of an electric mixer fitted with a whisk attachment. On medium speed whisk the egg whites slowly while adding the sugar syrup, aiming for the side of the bowl rather than the whisk. Once all the syrup is added, turn to the highest speed and keep whisking until the meringue becomes thick and glossy, for about 8–10 minutes. Make sure the meringue is still warm as it will be easier to work with.

Fill a piping (icing) bag fitted with a plain 1.5 cm (⅝ inch) nozzle, and pipe meringue as desired. Torch with a brûlée torch until lightly golden in colour. These tarts are best eaten on the day they are made.

Notes: The pastry cases can be made in advance and stored in an airtight container for up to 1 week. The passionfruit filling can be refrigerated for up to 1 week.

1 quantity Sweet Pastry (see page 218)

PASSIONFRUIT FILLING
200 g (7 oz) tin condensed milk
60 ml (2 fl oz/¼ cup) lemon juice
65 ml (2¼ fl oz) sieved passionfruit pulp
2 egg yolks, at room temperature

MERINGUE
330 g (11¾ oz/1½ cups) caster (superfine) sugar
pinch of cream of tartar
3 egg whites, at room temperature
½ teaspoon natural vanilla extract

This is a real show-off of a tart. When you crack through the brittle caramel to the sweet citrusy lemon and tartness of roasted rhubarb, it's a revelation. It is not mandatory to brûlée the tart, but certainly well worth the effort.

BAKED LEMON AND RHUBARB TARTS

1 quantity Sweet Pastry (see page 218)

3 rhubarb stalks, trimmed

3 tablespoons caster (superfine) sugar

600 ml (21 fl oz) Lemon Curd (see page 228)

icing (confectioners') sugar

Makes eight 10 cm tarts • **Preparation time** 40 minutes plus 30 minutes freezing time for pastry and setting time in fridge • **Cooking time** 45 minutes

Preheat the oven to 180°C (350°F). Lightly grease eight 10 cm (4 inch) round, loose-based fluted flan (tart) tins.

On a lightly floured surface, roll out the pastry to 3 mm (⅛ inch) thick. Line the tins and trim any excess pastry. Cover with plastic wrap and rest in the freezer for at least 30 minutes.

Line a baking tray with baking paper. Cut the rhubarb into 5 cm (2 inch) lengths, place on the baking tray and sprinkle over the caster sugar. Roast for approximately 10–15 minutes, until just soft enough to take the point of a knife. Allow to cool before using. Drain well on paper towel.

To blind bake the tart cases, line the tins with pieces of crumpled baking paper and pour in some baking beads or uncooked rice or dried beans. Bake for 10–15 minutes. Remove the paper and weights, return to the oven and bake until golden, approximately a further 10–15 minutes. Remove from the oven and allow to cool.

Place the rhubarb into the tart shells, spoon over the lemon curd and level with a palette knife. Put into the fridge until the curd sets.

Sift a thin, even layer of icing sugar over the lemon curd. Ignite a brûlée torch and with a slow sweeping motion guide the flame over the sugar. The nozzle should be 5–7.5 cm (2–3 inches) from the surface. The sugar will melt slowly at first then caramelise. Serve immediately.

Notes: You can bake the pastry cases in advance and store them in an airtight container for up to 1 week or freeze for up to 1 month. The lemon curd can also be made and refrigerated up to 2 weeks ahead.

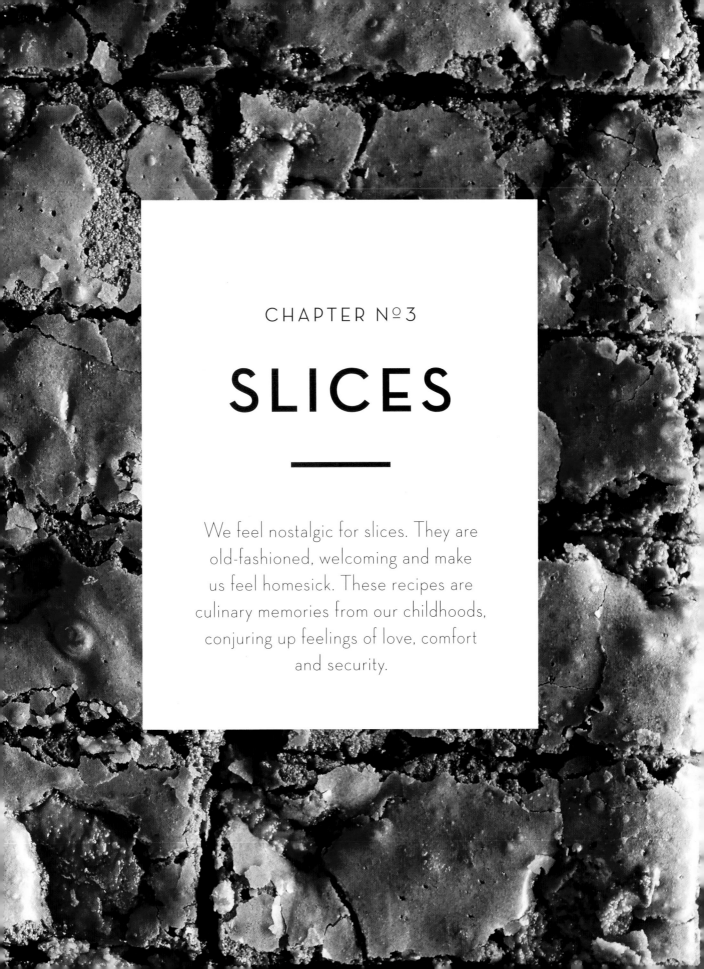

CHAPTER №3

SLICES

—

We feel nostalgic for slices. They are old-fashioned, welcoming and make us feel homesick. These recipes are culinary memories from our childhoods, conjuring up feelings of love, comfort and security.

The custard square is a classic bakery treat. To many Kiwis, the custard square rates right up there with the pavlova as a classic Kiwi icon. It consists of a thick layer of vanilla custard, sandwiched between two layers of buttery, flaky pastry and iced with a vanilla or passionfruit icing.

PASSIONFRUIT CUSTARD SQUARES

Makes 12 pieces • **Preparation time** 30 minutes • **Cooking time** 25 minutes

1 quantity Pie Top (see page 219)
3 quantities Vanilla Pastry Crème
    (see page 222)

ICING
250 g (9 oz/2 cups) icing
    (confectioners') sugar, sifted
2 tablespoons passionfruit pulp
1 tablespoon lemon juice

Preheat the oven to 180°C (350°F). Lightly grease two large baking trays.

Cut the pastry in half. On a lightly floured surface, roll out the pastry to form a rectangle 20 x 30 cm (8 x 12 inches). Repeat with the other half of the pastry.

Place them onto the prepared baking trays and prick all over with a fork. Cover each pastry sheet with a piece of baking paper and lay another baking tray on top to keep the pastry from rising.

Bake for 20–25 minutes or until dark golden brown. Remove from the oven, take off the top trays and baking paper and set aside to cool on a wire rack.

Lightly grease and line the base and sides of a 20 x 30 x 4 cm (8 x 12 x 1½ inch) slab tin with baking paper. Cut both sheets of the pastry to fit the prepared tin. Place one sheet of the pastry into the base of the tin. Fill with hot pastry crème, levelling out with a palette knife. Place the second piece of pastry on top, then allow to cool to room temperature before icing.

For the icing: In a small bowl mix together the sugar, passionfruit pulp and lemon juice.

Invert the custard square onto a clean tray, remove the baking paper and spread over the passionfruit icing. Let the icing set before cutting into squares. Cut into twelve 7 x 7.5 cm (2¾ x 3 inch) pieces.

These squares are best eaten on the day they are made.

This was one of Tass's mum's favourite slices to make, but it never lasted that long in the cake tin with a hungry husband and five growing kids. Not sure of the origin of this very distinct New Zealand recipe, but thanks Mum, it sure is a winner!

OATY GINGER CRUNCH

Makes eight pieces • **Preparation time** 25 minutes • **Cooking time** 35 minutes

Preheat the oven to 180°C (350°F). Lightly grease and line the base and sides of an 11 x 34 x 2.5 cm (4¼ x 13½ x 1 inch) rectangular loose-based baking tin with baking paper, cutting into the corners to fit and allowing the paper to extend about 2.5 cm (1 inch) above the sides.

For the base: Sift the flour, baking powder and ginger into a medium bowl, then add the coconut, rolled oats and brown sugar. In a small saucepan, melt the butter and golden syrup over low heat. Pour into the dry ingredients and mix until combined.

Press the base mixture into the prepared tin. Bake for 25–30 minutes or until golden brown.

For the icing: Sift the icing sugar and ginger into a small bowl. Melt the butter and golden syrup in a small saucepan over low heat. Mix into the sugar mixture until smooth and spread evenly over the cooked base with a large spatula. Leave to set in the tin before cutting (we leave it overnight).

Cut into eight 4.25 x 11 cm (1⅔ x 4¼ inch) pieces.

Note: This slice will keep for up to 3–4 days stored in an airtight container.

BASE

150 g (5½ oz/1 cup) plain (all-purpose) flour

1½ teaspoons baking powder

1½ teaspoons ground ginger

75 g (2¾ oz) desiccated coconut

165 g (5¾ oz/1⅔ cups) rolled (porridge) oats

150 g (5½ oz/¾ cup, lightly packed) light brown sugar

150 g (5½ oz) butter

70 g (2½ oz) golden syrup (light treacle)

ICING

290 g (10¼ oz/2⅓ cups) icing (confectioners') sugar

1 tablespoon ground ginger

120 g (4¼ oz) butter

115 g (4 oz/⅓ cup) golden syrup (light treacle)

Originally known as the Empire biscuit, but more commonly called the Belgian biscuit in New Zealand, our recipe is an old-fashioned spice biscuit slice with a raspberry jam centre. Traditionally, this is served for morning or afternoon tea.

BELGIAN SLICE

Makes 16 pieces • **Preparation time** 25 minutes plus 15 minutes chilling time for dough • **Cooking time** 30 minutes

Preheat the oven to 180°C (350°F). Lightly grease and line the base and sides of a 20 x 30 cm (8 x 12 inch) slab tin with baking paper.

Sift the flour, baking powder, salt and spices into a medium bowl.

Use an electric mixer fitted with a paddle attachment to beat the butter and sugar until pale and creamy. Add the eggs one at a time, mix well and then stir in the golden syrup and sifted dry ingredients. Mix until well combined.

Divide the dough into two portions, press one portion into the prepared tin. Flatten the second portion of dough, wrap in plastic wrap, and chill in the fridge for 15 minutes. Spread the raspberry jam over the base, then coarsely grate the chilled portion of dough over the jam.

Bake for 30 minutes or until golden brown. Allow to cool in the tin before slicing. Dust with icing sugar.

Using a sharp knife, cut into rectangles approximately 5 x 7.5 cm (2 x 3 inches) to make 16 pieces.

Note: This slice will keep for up to 3–4 days stored in an airtight container.

600 g (1 lb 5 oz/4 cups) plain (all-purpose) flour
1 tablespoon baking powder
½ teaspoon salt
1 tablespoon mixed spice
1 tablespoon ground ginger
220 g (7¾ oz) butter, softened
230 g (8 oz/1¼ cups, lightly packed) light brown sugar
2 eggs, at room temperature
2 tablespoons golden syrup (light treacle)

320 g (11¼ oz/1 cup) Raspberry Jam (see page 226)

icing (confectioners') sugar, to dust

73

SLICES

If you are in the mood for bananas and white chocolate, our blondie is the way to go. It's a really quick and easy dessert — try serving it hot with ice cream.

75

BANANA WHITE CHOCOLATE BLONDIE

Makes 16 pieces • **Preparation time** 20 minutes • **Cooking time** 40 minutes

350 g (12 oz/2⅓ cups) plain (all-purpose) flour

1½ teaspoons baking powder

½ teaspoon salt

150 g (5½ oz) butter, chopped

350 g (12 oz) white chocolate, chopped

245 g (8¾ oz/1⅓ cups, lightly packed) light brown sugar

2 eggs, at room temperature, lightly beaten

300 g (10½ oz/3 medium) bananas, mashed

2 teaspoons natural vanilla extract

45 g (1½ oz/½ cup) banana chips (optional)

Preheat the oven to 180°C (350°F). Lightly grease and line the base and sides of a 20 x 30 cm (8 x 12 inch) slab tin with baking paper.

Sift the flour, baking powder and salt into a medium bowl.

In a medium saucepan, melt the butter over low heat. Remove from the heat, add the white chocolate and stir until melted. Pour into a large bowl and add the sugar, eggs, mashed banana and vanilla, and mix well.

Fold through the sifted dry ingredients, mixing until well combined.

Pour into the prepared tin, then scatter over the banana chips, if using, and bake for 30–35 minutes until golden brown and just set. Allow to cool in the tin before slicing.

Using a sharp knife, cut into rectangles approximately 5 x 7.5 cm (2 x 3 inches) to make 16 pieces.

Note: This slice will keep for up to 3–4 days stored in an airtight container.

Our variation of the classic caramel slice has a modern twist — a crunchy polenta base, rich sticky caramel, all finished off with a sprinkling of sea salt flakes.

SALTED CARAMEL SLICE

Makes eight pieces • **Preparation time** 30 minutes • **Cooking time** 1 hour 10 minutes

Preheat the oven to 180°C (350°F). Lightly grease and line the base and sides of an 11 x 34 x 2.5 cm (4¼ x 13½ x 1 inch) rectangular loose-based baking tin with baking paper, cutting into the corners to fit and allowing the paper to extend about 2.5 cm (1 inch) above the sides.

For the base: Sift the sugar, polenta, flour and baking powder into a medium bowl, add the melted butter and mix until incorporated. The mixture will resemble fine breadcrumbs.

Press evenly into the prepared tin. Bake for 25–30 minutes until golden brown, then set aside.

For the filling: Combine the melted butter, golden syrup and condensed milk in a heavy-based saucepan, place over medium heat and stir constantly, especially scraping around the sides and edge of the pan to prevent sticking. Keep cooking and stirring for approximately 10–15 minutes until the mixture starts to thicken.

Pour over the base and spread evenly. Sprinkle with sea salt and bake for a further 20 minutes or until golden in colour. Leave to cool in the tin before slicing.

Cut into eight 4.25 x 11 cm (1⅔ x 4¼ inch) pieces.

Note: This slice will keep for up to 3–4 days stored in an airtight container.

BASE

185 g (6½ oz/1 cup, lightly packed) light brown sugar
130 g (4½ oz/⅔ cup) fine polenta
110 g (3¾ oz/¾ cup) self-raising flour
½ teaspoon baking powder
135 g (4¾ oz) butter, melted

FILLING

60 g (2¼ oz) butter, melted
90 g (3¼ oz/¼ cup) golden syrup (light treacle)
2 x 395 g (14 oz) tins condensed milk
½ teaspoon sea salt flakes

No cake or slice collection would be complete without a traditional Louise cake. Louise has a shortcake base, slathered with raspberry jam and topped with a delicately crisp coconut meringue.

This is Cherie's mother's recipe and it takes her back to coming home from school to the smell of home baking.

LOUISE CAKE

Makes 16 pieces • **Preparation time** 30 minutes • **Cooking time** 45 minutes

BASE

110 g (3¾ oz) butter, at room
    temperature
110 g (3¾ oz/½ cup) caster
    (superfine) sugar
3 egg yolks, at room temperature
juice of 1 lemon
225 g (8 oz/1½ cups) plain
    (all-purpose) flour
1 teaspoon baking powder

320 g (11¼ oz/1 cup) Raspberry Jam
    (see page 226)

TOPPING

6 egg whites, at room temperature
370 g (13 oz/1⅔ cups) caster
    (superfine) sugar
175 g (6 oz) desiccated coconut

Preheat the oven to 180°C (350°F). Lightly grease and line the base and sides of a 20 x 30 cm (8 x 12 inch) slab tin with baking paper.

For the base: Use an electric mixer fitted with a paddle attachment to beat the butter and sugar until pale and creamy. Add the egg yolks and lemon juice and continue mixing until combined. Sift in the flour and baking powder and mix on low until just combined.

Press evenly into the prepared tin. Spread over the raspberry jam and set aside.

For the topping: Use an electric mixer with a whisk attachment to whisk the egg whites to stiff peaks, then gradually whisk in the sugar. Fold through the coconut and spread the meringue evenly on top of the base.

Bake for 40–45 minutes until crisp and lightly golden. Leave to cool in the tin before slicing.

Using a sharp knife, cut into rectangles approximately 5 x 7.5 cm (2 x 3 inches) to make 16 pieces.

Note: This slice will keep for up to 3–4 days stored in an airtight container.

Who would have thought that a brownie could be so popular! This recipe came about by adding left-over caramel to our chocolate brownie recipe. And it's much quicker to make than a cake. A brownie should have the texture somewhere between a cake and a soft cookie.

CHOCOLATE SALTED CARAMEL BROWNIE

Makes 16 pieces • **Preparation time** 40 minutes • **Cooking time** 1 hour 15 minutes

Preheat the oven to 180°C (350°F). Line a 10 x 20 cm (4 x 8 inch) loaf (bar) tin with baking paper.

For the salted caramel: In a medium heavy-based saucepan, combine the butter, golden syrup and condensed milk. Stir constantly over medium heat, especially scraping around the side and edge of the saucepan to prevent sticking. Keep cooking until the mixture starts to thicken, approximately 10–15 minutes.

Pour into the lined tray and sprinkle with the sea salt. Bake for 15–20 minutes until golden brown. Leave to cool in the tin.

Lightly grease and line the base and sides of a 20 x 30 cm (8 x 12 inch) slab tin with baking paper.

For the brownie: Melt the butter in a medium saucepan over medium–low heat. Take off the heat and add the chocolate. Stir until melted and smooth, then set aside.

Use an electric mixer with a whisk attachment to whisk the eggs, vanilla and sugar until combined. Whisk in the melted butter and chocolate. Then fold in the sifted flour and salt and mix until smooth. Pour into the prepared tin. Dot evenly with pieces of caramel and bake for 25–30 minutes until just set.

Using a sharp knife, cut into rectangles approximately 5 x 7.5 cm (2 x 3 inches) to make 16 pieces.

Notes: To get a neat cut these can be made a day before and left to set overnight at room temperature. This slice will keep for up to 3–4 days stored in an airtight container.

Tip: You don't want to overcook the brownie. Unlike cakes, you don't want the skewer to come out clean. It should be set on the outside but still fudgy in the middle.

SALTED CARAMEL
30 g (1 oz) butter
45 g (1½ oz) golden syrup
   (light treacle)
1 x 395 g (14 oz) tin condensed milk
¼ teaspoon sea salt flakes

BROWNIE
375 g (13 oz) butter, chopped
375 g (13 oz/2½ cups) dark chocolate,
   chopped
6 eggs, at room temperature
1 teaspoon natural vanilla extract
495 g (1 lb 1½ oz/2¼ cups) caster
   (superfine) sugar
225 g (8 oz/1½ cups) plain
   (all-purpose) flour
1 teaspoon salt

On those days when you don't have time to make breakfast before leaving the house, a slice of this bar is a great breakfast on the run. It's full of oats, nuts, seeds, coconut, honey and fruits.

BREAKFAST BAR

JAM

140 g (5 oz/1½ cups) dried apples

105 g (3¾ oz/⅔ cup) dried cranberries

155 g (5½ oz/1 cup) dried apricots, diced

75 g (2¾ oz/⅓ cup) caster (superfine) sugar

BASE

95 g (3¼ oz/⅔ cup) walnut pieces, lightly toasted

250 g (9 oz/1⅔ cups) plain (all-purpose) flour

150 g (5½ oz/1½ cups) rolled (porridge) oats

150 g (5½ oz/¾ cup, lightly packed) light brown sugar

80 g (2¾ oz) thread (shredded) coconut

1 teaspoon salt

1 teaspoon ground cinnamon

230 g (8 oz) butter

130 g (4½ oz) honey

TOPPING

40 g (1½ oz/¼ cup) linseeds (flaxseeds)

55 g (2 oz/⅓ cup) sunflower seeds

50 g (1¾ oz/¼ cup) hulled millet

Makes 16 pieces • **Preparation time** 40 minutes plus cooling time for jam and chilling time for base mixture • **Cooking time** 1 hour 20 minutes

Preheat the oven to 180°C (350°F). Lightly grease and line the base and sides of a 20 x 30 cm (8 x 12 inch) slab tin with baking paper.

For the jam: In a food processor, pulse the dried apple to coarsely chop. In a medium saucepan over medium heat put the apples, cranberries, apricots, sugar and 450 ml (15¾ fl oz) water. Bring to a boil, then reduce the heat to low and simmer for 10 minutes or until the dried fruits have softened. Set aside to cool.

For the base: In a food processor, pulse the walnuts, flour, oats, brown sugar, coconut, salt and cinnamon to a coarse texture. Transfer to a large mixing bowl.

In a small saucepan, over low heat, melt the butter and honey together. Add the butter and honey to the dry ingredients and mix until the mixture is evenly combined.

Divide the mix into thirds and press two-thirds into the prepared tin then bake for 30 minutes or until golden brown. Place the remaining one-third in the fridge while the base is cooking.

Remove from the oven and leave to cool. Once cooled, spread the jam evenly over the base.

For the topping: Remove the reserved base mixture from the fridge and break up with your fingers into a small bowl. Add the linseeds, sunflower seeds and millet and stir until combined.

Crumble evenly over the base and jam. Return to the oven and bake for a further 30 minutes or until golden brown. Cool in the tin for 2–3 hours before slicing.

Using a sharp knife, cut into rectangles approximately 5 x 7.5 cm (2 x 3 inches) to make 16 pieces.

Notes: The jam can be made in advance and stored in the fridge for up to 2 weeks. This slice will keep for up to 5 days stored in an airtight container in the fridge.

Classic Kiwiana. A sweet malt biscuit fudge, packed with Fruit Puffs or Eskimos and coated in coconut. It is so easy! No baking is needed. It's an absolute childhood favourite.

NEW ZEALAND LOLLY CAKE

Makes 16 pieces • **Preparation time** 20 minutes • **Cooking time** 10 minutes

Lightly grease a 8 x 32 x 8 cm (3¼ x 12½ x 3¼ inch) loaf (bar) tin.

In a medium saucepan, over medium–low heat, warm the condensed milk, add the melted butter, then remove from the heat.

Mix through the biscuits and fruit puffs. Roll in the coconut and press into the prepared tin. Refrigerate until set.

Cut into sixteen 8 x 2 cm (3¼ x ¾ inch) slices.

Note: This slice will keep for up to 5–7 days stored in an airtight container in the fridge.

1 x 395 g (14 oz) tin condensed milk

200 g (7 oz) butter, melted

500 g (1 lb 2 oz/2 packets) malt biscuits, finely crushed

360 g (12¾ oz/5 cups) Fruit Puffs or Eskimos or coloured marshmallows, chopped

135 g (4¾ oz/1½ cups) desiccated coconut, for rolling

The combination of buttery shortbread and tangy lemon curd makes these shortbreads totally irresistible. You get equally impressive results using passionfruit curd.

LEMON CURD SHORTBREAD

500 g (1 lb 2 oz/3⅓ cups) plain
(all-purpose) flour

1 teaspoon salt

280 g (10 oz) butter, at room
temperature

220 g (7¾ oz/1 cup) caster
(superfine) sugar

1 teaspoon natural vanilla extract

600 g (1 lb 5 oz) Lemon Curd
(see page 228)

Makes 16 pieces • **Preparation time** 20 minutes plus chilling time for reserved dough and cooling time for base • **Cooking time** 55 minutes

Preheat the oven to 180°C (350°F). Lightly grease and line the base and sides of a 20 x 30 cm (8 x 12 inch) slab tin with baking paper.

In a bowl, sift together the flour and salt, and set aside. Use an electric mixer fitted with a paddle attachment to beat the butter, sugar and vanilla until pale and creamy. Add the sifted dry ingredients and bring together until a dough has formed.

Press two-thirds of the dough into the prepared tin, reserving the remaining one-third for the topping. Flatten the reserved dough, wrap in plastic wrap, and chill in the fridge while the base is baking.

Bake the base for 25 minutes or until golden brown. Remove from the oven and let cool in the tin.

Spread the cooled shortbread base with the lemon curd and evenly crumble or grate the chilled portion of dough over the lemon curd. Return to the oven and bake for a further 30 minutes or until golden brown. Cool in the tin.

Using a sharp knife, cut into rectangles approximately 5 x 7.5 cm (2 x 3 inches) to make 16 pieces.

Notes: The base can be made and baked the day before and the topping portion kept in the fridge so it is ready to finish off when required. This slice will keep for up to 3–4 days stored in an airtight container.

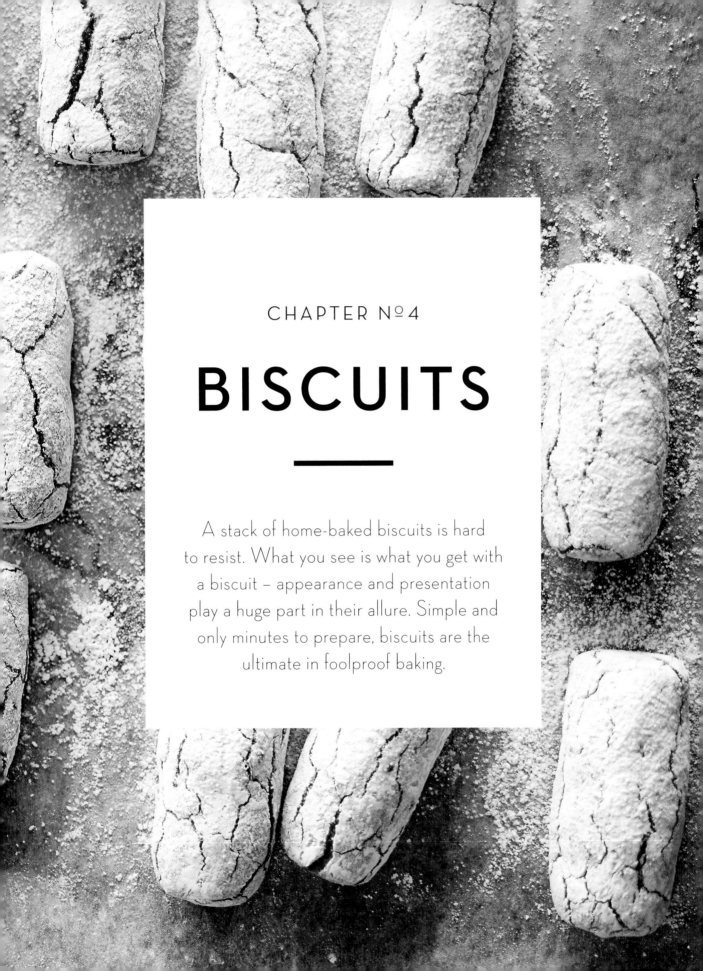

CHAPTER №4

BISCUITS

———

A stack of home-baked biscuits is hard
to resist. What you see is what you get with
a biscuit – appearance and presentation
play a huge part in their allure. Simple and
only minutes to prepare, biscuits are the
ultimate in foolproof baking.

Growing up, we knew these biscuits as peanut brownies and they were a school lunch box classic. Sandwiched with peanut butter cream, two halves make an even better whole!

PEANUT BUTTER COOKIES

Makes 12 • **Preparation time** 20 minutes • **Cooking time** 30 minutes

Preheat the oven to 180°C (350°F). Line two baking trays with baking paper.

Lightly roast the peanuts in a baking tin for 10 minutes. Set aside to cool, then roughly chop.

Sift together the flour, cocoa powder and baking powder.

Use an electric mixer fitted with a paddle attachment to beat the butter and sugar until pale and creamy. Add the eggs and mix well.

Add the sifted dry ingredients and mix until a dough forms. Add the peanuts and coconut and combine thoroughly.

Place tablespoonfuls of the dough on the prepared trays, leaving a 3 cm (1¼ inch) space between each biscuit to allow for spreading. Flatten slightly with a fork. Bake for 15–20 minutes, until firm to touch.

For the peanut butter cream: In the bowl of an electric mixer fitted with a paddle attachment, beat together the vanilla cream filling, ganache and peanut butter until well incorporated.

Allow the biscuits to cool completely on the tray. Sandwich together with generous amounts of the peanut butter cream.

Notes: Store unfilled biscuits in an airtight container for up to 5 days. Once filled, they are best eaten on the day.

280 g (10 oz/2 cups) raw blanched peanuts

250 g (9 oz/1⅔ cups) plain (all-purpose) flour

2 tablespoons cocoa powder

2 teaspoons baking powder

230 g (8 oz) butter, at room temperature

415 g (14¾ oz/2¼ cups, lightly packed) light brown sugar

2 eggs, at room temperature

150 g (5½ oz/1⅔ cups) desiccated coconut

PEANUT BUTTER CREAM

220 g (7¾ oz/1 cup) Vanilla Cream Filling (see page 94)

2 tablespoons Chocolate Ganache (see page 18)

2 tablespoons crunchy peanut butter

THE COOK AND BAKER

The name biscotti means 'twice-cooked'. Traditionally, biscotti were almond flavoured but your imagination is the only limiting factor to what can be added to these cookies — dried fruits, chocolates, nuts, seeds or spices ... experiment and enjoy!

CHOCOLATE ALMOND BISCOTTI

250 g (9 oz/1⅔ cups) plain
(all-purpose) flour
½ teaspoon baking powder
pinch of salt
165 g (5¾ oz/¾ cup) caster
(superfine) sugar
110 g (3¾ oz/⅔ cup) blanched
almonds
100 g (3½ oz/⅔ cup) dark chocolate,
chopped
2 eggs, at room temperature,
lightly beaten
¼ teaspoon natural vanilla extract
finely grated zest of ½ lemon

Makes 30–40 • **Preparation time** 30 minutes plus cooling time for dough • **Cooking time** 35 minutes

Preheat the oven to 180°C (350°F). Line a baking tray with baking paper.

Sift the flour, baking powder and salt into a medium bowl. Add the sugar, almonds and chocolate.

In a small bowl mix together the eggs, vanilla and lemon zest. Add to the dry ingredients and mix until combined.

Roll into a log 10 x 20 cm (4 x 8 inches), place on the prepared tray, and bake for 20 minutes until golden and firm. Leave to cool on the tray. Reduce the oven temperature to 160°C (315°F).

Cut the log into slices on a slight angle using a serrated knife, approximately 5 mm (¼ inch) in thickness. Place the slices on the baking tray and bake the biscotti for a further 10–15 minutes, until the biscuits have dried out. Leave on the tray to cool completely.

Notes: You can do the first bake and leave the log in the fridge for 1 week, then slice and do the second bake when needed, always having fresh biscotti on hand. The biscotti can be stored in an airtight container for up to 2 weeks.

This is our version of the world's favourite cookie. Do you split them and eat the filling first, eat them whole, or dunk them? One thing for sure is they should be served with a tall glass of cold milk.

COOKIES AND CREAM

Makes 16–18 • **Preparation time** 30 minutes plus 1 hour resting and chilling time for dough • **Cooking time** 20 minutes

Preheat the oven to 180°C (350°F). Line two baking trays with baking paper.

Use an electric mixer fitted with a whisk attachment to combine the melted butter and caster sugar. Whisk in the chocolate and egg until thoroughly incorporated.

In a medium bowl, sift together the flour, cocoa powder, salt and bicarbonate of soda. Fold into the chocolate mixture. You may need to mix by hand until the dough comes together. Leave to sit for approximately 1 hour to firm up.

Roll into a log, approximately 5 cm (2 inches) in diameter, wrap in baking paper and refrigerate until firm.

Cut the dough log into 1 cm (½ inch) thick slices and place on the prepared trays, 5 cm (2 inches) apart. Bake for 15–20 minutes until firm. Leave to cool completely on the trays.

For the cream filling: Use an electric mixer fitted with a paddle attachment to beat the butter and icing sugar until smooth. Add the vanilla, milk and salt and beat again until smooth and incorporated.

Sandwich the biscuits together with the cream.

Notes: The biscuit dough and the cream filling can be stored in the fridge for up to 1 week. Store unfilled biscuits in an airtight container for up to 5 days. Once filled, they are best eaten on the day.

230 g (8 oz) butter, melted and cooled
165 g (5¾ oz/¾ cup) caster (superfine) sugar
210 g (7½ oz) dark chocolate, melted and cooled slightly
1 egg, at room temperature, lightly beaten
225 g (8 oz/1½ cups) plain (all-purpose) flour
80 g (2¾ oz/¾ cup) dark cocoa powder
1 teaspoon salt
½ teaspoon bicarbonate of soda (baking soda)

VANILLA CREAM FILLING
120 g (4¼ oz) butter, softened
250 g (9 oz/2 cups) icing (confectioners') sugar
1 teaspoon natural vanilla extract
1 tablespoon milk
pinch of salt

This is a popular little Italian biscuit, which is crisp on the outside and slightly chewy on the inside. Made even more more-ish by adding dried apricots and mandarin zest.

APRICOT AND MANDARIN AMARETTI

180 g (6¼ oz/1¾ cups) almond meal

110 g (3¾ oz/½ cup) caster
    (superfine) sugar

finely grated zest of 1 mandarin

80 g (2¾ oz/½ cup) dried apricots,
    diced

2 egg whites, at room temperature

2 teaspoons honey

icing (confectioners') sugar, for rolling

Makes 20 • **Preparation time** 20 minutes • **Cooking time** 15 minutes

Preheat the oven to 180°C (350°F). Line a baking tray with baking paper.

In a medium bowl, mix the almond meal, caster sugar and mandarin zest. Rub together with your fingertips to disperse the zest evenly. Stir in the dried apricots.

Use an electric mixer with a whisk attachment to whisk the egg whites and honey until soft peaks form. Gently fold the egg whites into the almond mixture and mix until a soft paste forms.

Roll the mixture into 20 balls, completely cover with the icing sugar and shape each into a log approximately 4–5 cm (1½–2 inches) long.

Arrange on the prepared tray. Bake for 12–15 minutes, until lightly golden and chewy in the centre.

Leave to cool completely on the tray.

Note: These biscuits can be stored in an airtight container for up to 5 days.

These biscuits are the love child of the brownie and the cookie. Do not be tempted to over-bake as these biscuits should be fudgy like a brownie.
Best scoffed while warm and gooey!

BROOKIES

Makes approximately 24 • **Preparation time** 25 minutes • **Cooking time** 25 minutes

Preheat the oven to 180°C (350°F). Line two baking trays with baking paper.

In a small saucepan, melt the butter over low heat, add the chopped chocolate and stir until melted. Set aside and allow to cool slightly.

In a bowl, sift together the flour, baking powder and salt.

Use an electric mixer fitted with a whisk attachment to whisk the eggs on medium–high until foamy and lightly thickened, approximately 40 seconds.

Increase the speed to high and gradually add the sugar and the vanilla. Whisk until thick and pale. Reduce the speed and beat in the melted chocolate and butter until fully incorporated.

Change to a paddle attachment and on a low speed, gradually add the sifted flour mix, then the coarsely chopped chocolate, pecans and walnuts. Mix until evenly distributed.

Roll tablespoonfuls of the mixture into balls and place on the prepared trays 4 cm (1½ inches) apart.

Bake for 17–20 minutes, until the biscuits are set around the edges, the centre will still be underdone. Do not over-bake. Leave to cool completely on the trays.

Note: These biscuits can be stored in an airtight container for up to 3 days.

125 g (4½ oz) butter
600 g (1 lb 5 oz/4 cups) dark chocolate, divided: 300 g (10½ oz/2 cups) chopped and 300 g (10½ oz/2 cups) coarsely chopped
100 g (3½ oz/⅔ cup) plain (all-purpose) flour
½ teaspoon baking powder
¼ teaspoon salt
3 eggs, at room temperature
275 g (9¾ oz/1¼ cups) caster (superfine) sugar
2 teaspoons natural vanilla extract
150 g (5½ oz/1½ cups) pecans, coarsely chopped
115 g (4 oz/1 cup) walnuts, coarsely chopped

These rich, fine-textured, buttery biscuits are so named because they seem to literally melt in your mouth in a moment. They are also known as a Yoyo.

PASSIONFRUIT MELTING MOMENTS

250 g (9 oz) butter, softened

90 g (3¼ oz/¾ cup) icing
   (confectioners') sugar

finely grated zest of 1 orange

½ teaspoon natural vanilla extract

60 g (2¼ oz/½ cup) cornflour
   (cornstarch)

250 g (9 oz/1⅔ cups) plain
   (all-purpose) flour

½ teaspoon salt

PASSIONFRUIT FILLING

120 g (4¼ oz) butter, softened

340 g (12 oz/2¾ cups) icing
   (confectioners') sugar, sifted

4 tablespoons passionfruit pulp,
   sieved

icing (confectioners') sugar,
   to dust

Makes 12–15 • **Preparation time** 30 minutes plus 30 minutes resting time for dough • **Cooking time** 15 minutes

Preheat the oven to 160°C (315°F). Line two baking trays with baking paper.

Use an electric mixer fitted with a paddle attachment to beat the butter and sugar until pale and creamy. Add the orange zest and vanilla and continue to beat. Sift in the cornflour, flour and salt and mix until combined.

Let this rest for 30 minutes to allow the mixture to firm up, making it easier to roll. Roll tablespoonfuls of dough into balls and place on the prepared trays 4 cm (1½ inches) apart. Flatten the tops slightly with a fork. Bake for approximately 10–15 minutes until firm, but not coloured. Leave to cool on the baking trays.

To make the passionfruit filling: Use an electric mixer with a beater attachment to beat the butter and sugar until pale and creamy. Then mix in the passionfruit pulp until smooth and incorporated.

Once the biscuits have cooled, sandwich them together with a generous amount of filling. Dust lightly with icing sugar.

Notes: You can bake the biscuits in advance, store in an airtight container for 3–4 days and fill when needed. Once filled, they are best eaten within 2–3 days.

Every Kiwi kid's induction into the kitchen to learn to bake was the Afghan. A buttery chocolate and cornflake biscuit, this combination of simple ingredients should not taste this good.

Thank you to Suzanne Watson from Christchurch for this recipe.

AFGHANS

Makes 18–20 • **Preparation time** 30 minutes • **Cooking time** 30 minutes

Preheat the oven to 160°C (315°F). Line a baking tray with baking paper.

In a bowl, sift together the flour and cocoa powder.

Use an electric mixer fitted with a paddle attachment to beat the butter and caster sugar until pale and creamy. Add the sifted dry ingredients and mix well.

Remove the bowl from the mixer and stir through the cornflakes with a wooden spoon, so the cornflakes don't crush up too much.

Place heaped tablespoonfuls on the prepared tray, leaving a 5 cm (2 inch) space between the biscuits. Do not flatten. Bake for 15–20 minutes, until they start to feel firm when pressed lightly in the centre. Allow to cool completely on the tray.

For the walnut praline: Arrange the walnuts on a baking tray lined with baking paper. In a medium saucepan, combine 2 tablespoons (1¼ fl oz/ 40 ml) water and the sugar. Bring to the boil, without stirring, over medium heat until the sugar dissolves. Then keep on cooking until golden amber in colour. Quickly pour the toffee over the nuts to coat. Allow to set and cool then break into shards.

For the chocolate icing: Sift together the icing sugar and cocoa powder into a bowl. Add the softened butter, vanilla and enough of the hot water to make an icing consistency.

Spoon a good dollop of icing onto each biscuit and top with roughly chopped walnut praline.

Notes: Best eaten within 1–2 days. The praline can be made and stored, broken into pieces, in an airtight container for up to 2 weeks.

250 g (9 oz/1⅔ cups) plain (all-purpose) flour

40 g (1½ oz/⅓ cup) dark cocoa powder

300 g (10½ oz) butter, at room temperature

110 g (3¾ oz/½ cup) caster (superfine) sugar

150 g (5½ oz/5 cups) cornflakes

WALNUT PRALINE
140 g (5 oz/1 cup) walnut pieces

220 g (7¾ oz/1 cup) caster (superfine) sugar

CHOCOLATE ICING
375 g (13 oz/3 cups) icing (confectioners') sugar

4 tablespoons cocoa powder

100 g (3½ oz) butter, softened

1 teaspoon natural vanilla extract

80 ml (2½ fl oz/⅓ cup) hot water, to mix

This recipe is for all the people who long for something healthy. Sugar free, dairy free and gluten free, you will be surprised at how incredibly rich and satisfying these are.

RAW BROWNIE

325 g (11½ oz/2⅓ cups) walnut pieces

100 g (3½ oz/1½ cups) thread (shredded) coconut

550 g (1 lb 4 oz) fresh medjool dates, pitted

80 g (2¾ oz/¾ cup) raw cacao powder

100 ml (3½ fl oz) coconut oil

desiccated coconut or raw cacao powder, to coat (optional)

Makes approximately 24 • **Preparation time** 20 minutes • **Cooking time** nil

Line a baking tray with baking paper.

Place the walnuts and coconut thread in the bowl of a food processor, and process until the walnuts and coconut are small and crumbly.

Add the remaining ingredients to the food processor. Process again until the mixture turns a lovely dark chocolate brown. Do not over-process or the mix will become too oily.

Roll into walnut-sized balls, roll in desiccated coconut or raw cacao powder, if using, and refrigerate to firm on the prepared tray.

Note: These brownies can be stored in an airtight container for up to 1 week.

Cherie's Nana inspired her to cook from when she was a very young girl, so one of her recipes had to feature in the book.

This shortbread is a very easy, simple recipe with ingredients that are always to hand.

NANA BARKER'S SHORTBREAD

Makes 24–30 • **Preparation time** 25 minutes plus 30 minutes chilling time for dough • **Cooking time** 30 minutes

Preheat the oven to 160°C (315°F).

Line a large baking tray with baking paper.

Sift the flour, icing sugar and salt into the bowl of an electric mixer fitted with a paddle attachment. Add the butter and mix on medium speed until it all comes together.

Shape into two logs, approximately 4 cm (1½ inches) in diameter. Wrap in plastic wrap and chill in the fridge for approximately 30 minutes to firm up before slicing into 8 mm (⅜ inch) thick slices.

Place onto the prepared tray 3 cm (1¼ inches) apart, prick them with a fork and bake for approximately 25–30 minutes until slightly golden. Allow to cool on the tray until firm.

Notes: The dough can be made ahead and stored in the freezer for up to 1 month. The shortbread can be stored in an airtight container for up to 1 week.

500 g (1 lb 2 oz/3⅓ cups) plain (all-purpose) flour
185 g (6½ oz/1½ cups) icing (confectioners') sugar
½ teaspoon salt
350 g (12 oz) butter, cold and diced

THE COOK AND BAKER

There are people who consider dunking déclassé, rude even. Pity them! The ultimate dunker is a classic biscuit with an incredibly robust, sweet and spicy flavour.

GINGERNUT DUNKERS

300 g (10½ oz/2 cups) plain (all-purpose) flour

3 teaspoons ground ginger

1 teaspoon mixed spice

¼ teaspoon bicarbonate of soda (baking soda)

¼ teaspoon salt

150 g (5½ oz) butter, at room temperature

275 g (9¾ oz/1¼ cups) caster (superfine) sugar

1 egg, at room temperature

350 g (12 oz/1 cup) golden syrup (light treacle)

100 g (3½ oz) demerara or raw sugar, for rolling

Makes 24–30 • **Preparation time** 20 minutes • **Cooking time** 15 minutes

Preheat the oven to 180°C (350°F). Line two baking trays with baking paper.

Sift together the flour, ginger, mixed spice, bicarbonate of soda and salt.

Use an electric mixer fitted with a paddle attachment to beat the butter and caster sugar until pale and creamy. Add the egg and golden syrup, and mix until well combined. Add the sifted dry ingredients and mix until just incorporated.

Roll into walnut-sized balls, coat in the demerara sugar, and place on the prepared baking trays. Flatten with the back of a fork, leaving a 2–3 cm (¾–1¼ inch) gap between each to allow for spreading. Bake for 15 minutes or until the biscuits are firm. Leave to cool and firm up on the trays.

Note: These biscuits can be stored in an airtight container for up to 1 week.

The greatest buttery biscuit there is, these almond shortbreads will become a favourite! Fill with your jam of choice, or our lemon or passionfruit curd.

BERRY JAM SHORTBREADS

Makes 24 • **Preparation time** 20 minutes • **Cooking time** 20 minutes

Preheat the oven to 170°C (325°F). Lightly grease a 24-hole 4 cm (1½ inch) mini muffin tin.

Sift the flour, cornflour and icing sugar together into the bowl of an electric mixer fitted with a paddle attachment, then stir in the almond meal. Add the butter, and mix until a dough forms. Do not overmix.

Roll into 24 small balls and place in the prepared muffin tin. Bake for approximately 15–20 minutes until lightly golden.

Remove from the oven and while still hot make a small indentation on top of each shortbread using the cylindrical handle of a wooden spoon. Cool for 10 minutes then turn out onto a wire rack. When completely cool, dust with the extra icing sugar and then fill with a small dollop of jam.

Once filled, these are best eaten on the day they are made.

Notes: You can use any jam for these. Also, you can store the unfilled shortbreads in an airtight container for 3–4 days and fill with jam as required before serving.

185 g (6½ oz/1¼ cups) plain (all-purpose) flour

60 g (2¼ oz/½ cup) cornflour (cornstarch)

90 g (3¼ oz/¾ cup) icing (confectioners') sugar, plus extra to dust

35 g (1¼ oz/⅓ cup) almond meal

250 g (9 oz) cold butter, chopped

320 g (11¼ oz/1 cup) Raspberry or Berry Jam (see page 226)

CHAPTER 5

DONUTS
AND MORE

—

Donuts are the new cupcakes, and you can kiss the trendy macaron goodbye. There is one recipe in action throughout this chapter: brioche is a traditional French bread and it's the foundation for many of our sweet and savoury pastries.

Donuts are a childhood favourite. The memory of your first cinnamon donut fresh from the fryer and tossed in sugar and spice stays with you forever. These are rings of golden promise! The best donuts are prepared by hand.

CINNAMON DONUTS

Makes 12 • **Preparation time** 20 minutes plus 30 minutes proving time for dough • **Cooking time** 25 minutes

Lightly grease a baking tray. Empty the brioche dough from the bowl onto a lightly floured surface. Divide the dough into 12 portions, and roll each portion into a taut bun. Place on the prepared tray, leaving plenty of room between them so they don't stick together while proving. Loosely cover with plastic wrap and leave in a warm place to prove, approximately 30 minutes until the dough has almost doubled in size.

In a large bowl, mix together the cinnamon and sugar. Put aside for coating the donuts once they are cooked.

In a deep-fryer or a medium saucepan, heat 5 cm (2 inches) of vegetable oil to 160°C (315°F), using a thermometer. When using hot oil, be extremely careful – do not leave unattended!

To shape the donuts, gently remove a bun from the tray. Taking care not to deflate the dough, pinch your thumb and index finger through the centre and carefully stretch the hole – being careful not to tear the rim – until the hole measures about 4 cm (1½ inches) in diameter. The hole will shrink when the donuts are frying.

Do not overcrowd the deep-fryer – fry only 3 or 4 at a time for 3 minutes on each side or until golden brown. Carefully remove the donuts from the deep-fryer and drain well on paper towel. Toss through the cinnamon sugar while still hot.

Best eaten warm or within 2–3 hours.

1 quantity Brioche Dough
(see page 124)

CINNAMON SUGAR
2 tablespoons ground cinnamon
350 g (12 oz/2 cups) rapadura (panela)
sugar or caster (superfine) sugar

vegetable oil, for deep-frying

To eat one of these tear apart the soft brioche exterior to reveal the luscious diplomat crème and home-made raspberry jam. This will certainly take you back to your school days.

VANILLA CUSTARD DONUTS

1 quantity Brioche Dough
   (see page 124)
vegetable oil, for deep-frying
Diplomat Crème (see page 223)
165 g (5¾ oz/½ cup) Raspberry Jam
   (see page 226)
sifted icing (confectioners') sugar,
   to coat

Makes 12 • **Preparation time** 30 minutes plus 30 minutes proving time for dough • **Cooking time** 25 minutes

Lightly grease a baking tray. Empty the brioche dough from the bowl onto a lightly floured surface. Divide the dough into 12 portions, and roll each portion into a taut bun. Place on the prepared tray, leaving plenty of room between them so they don't stick together while proving. Loosely cover with plastic wrap and leave in a warm place to prove, approximately 30 minutes until the dough has almost doubled in size.

In a deep-fryer or a medium saucepan, heat 5 cm (2 inches) of vegetable oil to 160°C (315°F), using a thermometer. When using hot oil, be extremely careful – do not leave unattended!

Gently remove the buns from the tray, taking care not to deflate the dough. Do not overcrowd the deep-fryer – fry only 3 or 4 at a time for 3 minutes on each side or until golden brown. Remove the donuts from the deep-fryer and drain well on paper towel. Set aside and allow to cool completely before filling.

Fill a piping (icing) bag fitted with a wide 1.5 cm (⅛ inch), plain nozzle with the diplomat crème. Roll each donut in icing sugar. With a small serrated knife make a cut halfway through the donut. Fill with a dollop of jam, and generously pipe diplomat crème into each donut. Dust with extra icing sugar.

Best eaten within 3–4 hours.

A dark-hued sinful beast filled with more-ish chocolate custard, salty caramel and dredged in cocoa powder and icing sugar, there is no turning back after one of these.

CHOCOLATE CUSTARD BRONUTS

Makes 12 • **Preparation time** 30 minutes plus 30 minutes proving time for dough • **Cooking time** 25 minutes

Lightly grease a baking tray. Empty the brioche dough from the bowl onto a lightly floured surface. Divide the dough into 12 portions, and roll each portion into a taut bun. Place on the prepared tray, leaving plenty of room between them so they don't stick together while proving. Loosely cover with plastic wrap and leave in a warm place to prove, approximately 30 minutes until the dough has almost doubled in size.

In a deep-fryer or a medium saucepan, heat 5 cm (2 inches) of vegetable oil to 160°C (315°F), using a thermometer. When using hot oil, be extremely careful – do not leave unattended!

Gently remove the buns from the tray, taking care not to deflate the dough. Do not overcrowd the deep-fryer – fry only 3 or 4 at a time for 3 minutes on each side or until golden brown. Remove the donuts from the deep-fryer and drain well on paper towel. Set aside and allow to cool completely before filling.

Sift together the cocoa powder and icing sugar. Roll each donut in the icing sugar and cocoa mixture. Fill a piping (icing) bag fitted with a wide 1.5 cm (⅝ inch), plain nozzle with chocolate diplomat crème. With a small serrated knife make a cut halfway through the donut. Fill with a heaped teaspoonful of salted caramel and generously pipe chocolate diplomat crème into each donut. Dust with the remaining icing sugar and cocoa mixture.

Best eaten within 3–4 hours.

1 quantity Brioche Dough
   (see page 124)
vegetable oil, for deep-frying
1 tablespoon cocoa powder, to dust
125 g (4½ oz/1 cup) icing
   (confectioners') sugar, to dust
1 quantity Chocolate Diplomat
   Crème (see page 223)
125 ml (4 fl oz/½ cup) Salted Caramel
   (see page 223)

This is a great Sunday brunch brioche. We use fresh blackberries to cut through the sweet lemon curd and rich, buttery bread. It's best to use fresh blackberries when in season, but you can substitute with frozen.

BLACKBERRY AND LEMON BRIOCHE

1 quantity Brioche Dough
   (see page 124)
1 quantity Lemon Curd (see page 228)
250 g (9 oz) fresh or frozen
   blackberries
165 g (5¾ oz/½ cup) apricot jam,
   to glaze
50 g (1¾ oz) pistachio kernels,
   chopped

Makes 12 • **Preparation time** 20 minutes plus 30 minutes proving time for dough • **Cooking time** 20 minutes

Preheat the oven to 180°C (350°F). Lightly grease twelve 9 cm (3½ inch) round, loose-based fluted flan (tart) tins.

Empty the brioche dough from the bowl onto a lightly floured surface. Divide the dough into 12 portions and roll each portion into a ball, then shape each one into a disc that fits into the prepared tins and place in the tins.

Loosely cover with plastic wrap. Leave in a warm place to prove, approximately 30 minutes until the dough has almost doubled in size.

Make a slight indentation in the dough. Spoon 1 tablespoon of lemon curd into the centre of each brioche. Dot over the blackberries and bake for 15–20 minutes until puffy and golden. Remove from the oven. Let cool, then remove from the tins.

Gently heat the apricot jam in a small saucepan, then pour through a sieve into a bowl.

Glaze with the melted jam and finish with the chopped pistachios.

Best eaten on the day they are made.

Warm from the oven, the cinnamon sugar or chocolate spread brioche is a perfect way to start the day.

GOOD MORNING BRIOCHE

Makes 12 • **Preparation time** 30 minutes plus 40 minutes first proving time for dough and 30 minutes second proving • **Cooking time** 30 minutes

Warm the milk in a small saucepan over low heat until it is lukewarm, then stir in the yeast, sugar and eggs.

Put the flour and salt in the bowl of an electric mixer fitted with a dough hook. Add the wet mixture to the flour and mix until a loose dough has formed. Increase the speed to medium–high and mix for 5 minutes. Add the softened butter and mix until it is incorporated and the dough becomes smooth and elastic, approximately 5 minutes.

Place the dough in a large greased bowl. Cover with plastic wrap and leave in a warm place until it has doubled in volume, approximately 40 minutes. Your dough is now ready to use.

Preheat the oven to 180°C (350°F). Line a 12-hole standard 250 ml (9 fl oz/1 cup) muffin tin with paper cases.

Empty the dough from the bowl onto a lightly floured surface. Roll the dough into a rectangle, approximately 25 x 48 cm (10 x 19 inches), and around 1 cm (½ inch) thick. At this point, you can make the chocolate or cinnamon sugar variations.

VARIATIONS

Chocolate Spread: Cover the dough with 450 g (1 lb/1½ cups) chocolate hazelnut spread, such as Nutella. Roll from the longest side to form a log. Slice into twelve 4 cm (1½ inch) thick slices, and place in the prepared tin. Loosely cover with plastic wrap. Leave in a warm place to prove, until the dough has almost doubled in size, about 30 minutes. Bake for 20–25 minutes until golden brown. Leave in the tin for 5 minutes before turning out.

Cinnamon Sugar: Thinly spread 150 g (5½ oz) of softened butter over the dough, then sprinkle liberally with 175 g (6 oz) Cinnamon Sugar (see page 114). Roll from the longest side to form a log. Slice into twelve 4 cm (1½ inch) thick slices, and place in the prepared tin. Loosely cover with plastic wrap. Leave in a warm place to prove, until the dough has almost doubled in size, about 30 minutes. Bake for 20–25 minutes until golden brown. Leave in the tin for 5 minutes before turning out.

BRIOCHE DOUGH

250 ml (9 fl oz/1 cup) full-cream (whole) milk

10 g (¼ oz/2 teaspoons) dried yeast

75 g (2¾ oz/⅓ cup) caster (superfine) sugar

2 eggs, at room temperature, lightly beaten

485 g (1 lb 1 oz/3¼ cups) plain (all-purpose) flour

1 teaspoon salt

75 g (2¾ oz) butter, cut into small pieces, softened

A classic summer combo — juicy ripe tomatoes, creamy goat's cheese and pungent basil. This brioche makes the perfect lunch when paired with a salad of mixed leaves.

TOMATO, BASIL AND GOAT'S CHEESE BRIOCHE

1 quantity Brioche Dough
(see page 124)

**TOMATO, BASIL AND
GOAT'S CHEESE TOPPING**
48 cherry tomatoes
olive oil, to drizzle
dijon mustard, to spread
250 g (9 oz) goat's cheese
200 g (7 oz) basil pesto
basil leaves, to garnish

Makes 12 • **Preparation time** 30 minutes plus 30 minutes proving time for dough • **Cooking time** 30 minutes

Preheat the oven to 180°C (350°F). In a roasting tin, put the cherry tomatoes and prick them once or twice with a sharp knife, then drizzle with a little olive oil. Roast for 8–10 minutes until softened. Set aside to cool.

Line a baking tray with baking paper or lightly grease twelve 10 cm (4 inch) flan (tart) tins.

Empty the brioche dough from the bowl onto a lightly floured surface. Divide the dough into 12 portions and roll each portion into a ball. With a rolling pin, roll each ball into a disc that fits into the tins, or roll slightly thinner if making free-form, and place on the prepared tray.

Loosely cover with plastic wrap. Leave in a warm place to prove, approximately 30 minutes until the dough has almost doubled in size. Make a slight indentation in the dough to layer over the topping.

For the topping: Spread a thin layer of dijon mustard over each dough base leaving a border. Top each with 4 roasted cherry tomatoes, and crumble over the goat's cheese.

Bake for 15–20 minutes until puffy and golden. Remove from the tins, then dot with some basil pesto and finish with a few leaves of basil and a drizzle of olive oil.

Serve hot or at room temperature. These can be reheated at 180°C (350°F) for 5–6 minutes or until warm.

Best eaten on the day they are made.

For your carnivorous friends, drape thinly sliced prosciutto over the baked brioche and finish off with a drizzle of olive oil. These are best made when figs are at their peak.

FIG, TALEGGIO, WALNUT AND CARAMELISED ONION BRIOCHE

Makes 12 • **Preparation time** 30 minutes plus 30 minutes proving time for dough • **Cooking time** 20 minutes

Preheat the oven to 180°C (350°F). Line a baking tray with baking paper or lightly grease twelve 10 cm (4 inch) flan (tart) tins.

Empty the brioche dough from the bowl onto a lightly floured surface. Divide the dough into 12 portions and roll each portion into a ball. With a rolling pin, roll each ball into a disc that fits into the tins, or roll slightly thinner if making free-form, and place on the prepared tray.

Loosely cover with plastic wrap. Leave in a warm place to prove, approximately 30 minutes until the dough has almost doubled in size. Make a slight indentation in the dough to layer over the topping.

For the topping: Spread a thin layer of dijon mustard over each dough base leaving a border. Top with two pieces of fig, a slice of taleggio, strew over some caramelised onions and finish with the chopped walnuts.

Bake for 15–20 minutes until puffy and golden. Remove from the tins, then drizzle with some olive oil to finish.

Serve hot or at room temperature. These can be reheated at 180°C (350°F) for 5–6 minutes or until warm.

Best eaten on the day they are made.

1 quantity Brioche Dough
(see page 124)

FIG, TALEGGIO, WALNUT AND CARAMELISED ONION TOPPING
dijon mustard, to spread
12 fresh figs, halved
250 g (9 oz) taleggio cheese
125 g (4½ oz/½ cup) Caramelised
Onion (see page 229)
60 g (2¼ oz/½ cup) walnuts,
roughly chopped
olive oil, to drizzle

Braided challah is a symbol of the Jewish Sabbath. It is customary to begin the Friday night meal with the head of the household reciting a blessing over this soft, rich, eggy bread.

CHALLAH

850 g (1 lb 14 oz/5⅔ cups) plain (all-purpose) flour

1 tablespoon salt

400 ml (14 fl oz) warm water

15 g (½ oz/3 teaspoons) dried yeast

110 g (3¾ oz/½ cup) caster (superfine) sugar

50 g (1¾ oz) honey

3 eggs, at room temperature, lightly beaten, plus 1 extra, beaten for glazing

100 ml (3½ fl oz) vegetable oil

sesame seeds and poppy seeds, for sprinkling (optional)

Makes 3 loaves • **Preparation time** 30 minutes plus 30 minutes first proving time for dough and 45 minutes second proving • **Cooking time** 25 minutes

Preheat the oven to 160°C (315°F). Line two baking trays with baking paper.

Sift the flour and salt into the bowl of an electric mixer fitted with a dough hook. Put the warm water into a small bowl, and mix in the yeast, sugar, honey, the 3 beaten eggs and the vegetable oil. Pour this into the flour and salt. Mix on medium speed for 8 minutes until smooth and elastic.

Place the dough into a large greased bowl, cover with plastic wrap and leave in a warm place to double in size, approximately 30 minutes. Place the dough onto a lightly floured surface, and divide it into three equal portions (to make three loaves).

Start with one portion of dough (keeping the other pieces covered with a tea towel/dish towel). Divide the dough into three equal pieces, then roll each piece into a long rope. This should be thick in the centre and tapered at the ends. Align the ropes side by side and start braiding. When you reach the end, pinch to seal and tuck the ends under the loaf. Repeat with the two remaining portions of dough.

Place the loaves onto the prepared trays, and loosely cover with plastic wrap. Leave in a warm place for 30–45 minutes until soft, puffy and almost doubled in size.

Brush each loaf with the extra beaten egg, then leave plain or sprinkle with sesame and/or poppy seeds. Bake for 20–25 minutes until golden brown. They will sound hollow when tapped on the base. Cool completely on a wire rack.

Best eaten on the day they are made or within 3 days if toasting.

Note: These loaves make the best French toast.

DONUTS AND MORE

These scones are one of the first savoury items from the oven every morning, and not a day goes by without Tass wanting to demolish one of these laden with butter. It's a battle for our fit, healthy baker!

CHEDDAR AND SWEETCORN SCONES

Makes 12–15 • **Preparation time** 20 minutes • **Cooking time** 25 minutes

Preheat the oven to 180°C (350°F). Line a baking tray with baking paper.

Sift the flour, salt and baking powder into a medium bowl. Rub the butter in until it resembles fine breadcrumbs. Mix through the cheddar, parmesan and spring onion.

In a bowl, mix the corn into the milk, then pour into the dry ingredients. Mix quickly to a soft dough. Do not overmix.

Tip the dough onto a lightly floured surface and pat it into a 3 cm (1¼ inch) thick round. Using a 7 cm (2¾ inch) round cutter, cut out the scones. Press the scraped dough together gently and cut out the remaining scones.

Place the scones on the prepared baking tray, 2 cm (¾ inch) apart, and sprinkle the tops with extra grated cheese.

Bake for 20–25 minutes, until golden brown and well risen. Cool on a wire rack. Serve with lashings of butter.

Best eaten on the day they are made.

Note: These are great toasted.

485 g (1 lb 1 oz/3¼ cups) plain (all-purpose) flour

¼ teaspoon salt

1 tablespoon baking powder

50 g (1¾ oz) butter, chopped, plus extra, to serve

100 g (3½ oz/1 cup) grated cheddar cheese, plus extra, for topping

30 g (1 oz/⅓ cup) coarsely grated parmesan

2 spring onions (scallions), thinly sliced

200 g (7 oz) tinned creamed corn

275 ml (9¾ fl oz) milk

CHAPTER Nº 6

FESTIVE BAKING

—

Some of our best recipes for special occasions have been passed down from one generation to the next, adapted, polished and preserved like family heirlooms. The holidays are a great time to make, create, give, share and EAT!

A recipe surrounded with contentious debate whether its origin is Australia or New Zealand. Either way, we love the pavlova for its crunchy, crisp exterior and its soft marshmallowy inside. It has everything a dessert should have without being too heavy.

PAVLOVA WREATH

Serves 8–10 • **Makes** one 30 cm pavlova wreath • **Preparation time** 50 minutes • **Cooking time** 1 hour 10 minutes plus cooling time

8 egg whites, at room temperature
600 g (1 lb 5 oz) caster (superfine) sugar
300 ml (10½ fl oz) Vanilla Whipped Cream (see page 221), to decorate
750 g (1 lb 10 oz) mixed fresh berries

Preheat the oven to 150°C (300°F). Line a large baking tray with baking paper. With a pencil, draw a large circle approximately 30 cm (12 inches) in diameter, then draw a second circle measuring 10 cm (4 inches) in the middle. Turn the paper pencil-side down on the tray.

Put the egg whites and sugar in a large bowl over a saucepan of simmering water, making sure the bowl doesn't touch the water, and stir for about 5–7 minutes, until the sugar is dissolved. At this stage the mixture will be warm.

Pour the mixture into the bowl of an electric mixer fitted with a whisk attachment. Whisk the egg white and sugar mixture until thick and the mixture has cooled, approximately 10–15 minutes.

Spoon onto the prepared tray and shape into a wreath using the circles as a guide.

Turn the oven temperature down to 100°C (200°F) and place the pavlova wreath in the oven. Bake for 1 hour. Turn the oven off and leave the wreath in the oven to cool completely.

Top with lashings of vanilla whipped cream and copious amounts of mixed berries.

Note: The pavlova can be made a day in advance; make sure it is kept in a cool dry place.

This pudding represents the essence of Christmas to us. Packed with berries and a hint of vanilla, it is the perfect dessert for our hot summer months. You will be surprised at how easy it is to make. Serve with a generous amount of crème anglaise.

SUMMER BERRY PUDDING

Serves 8–10 • **Makes** one large pudding • **Preparation time** 40 minutes plus cooling time for berries and overnight refrigeration • **Cooking time** 10 minutes

BERRY COMPOTE

1 vanilla bean

195 g (6¾ oz/1½ cups) frozen blackberries

310 g (11 oz/2½ cups) frozen blueberries

220 g (7¾ oz/1 cup) caster (superfine) sugar

625 g (1 lb 6 oz/5 cups) frozen raspberries

½ loaf sliced white sandwich bread, crusts removed

1 quantity Crème Anglaise, to serve (see page 224)

Split the vanilla bean in half lengthways and scrape the seeds from the pods with the tip of a sharp knife. Keep the seeds.

In a large stainless steel saucepan, combine the blackberries, blueberries, sugar and vanilla bean seeds and bring slowly to the boil. Stir in the raspberries then remove from the heat. Set aside to cool.

When cooled, strain 250 ml (9 fl oz/1 cup) of the liquid from the berries and put aside.

Line a 1.5 litre (52 fl oz/6 cup) pudding basin with plastic wrap, leaving enough overhang to cover the pudding completely.

Reserve three slices of bread and cut the remaining slices in half. Dip one side of the bread into the strained berry juices. Line the base and sides of the pudding basin, soaked side facing out, overlapping the bread as you go.

Put aside 250 ml (9 fl oz/1 cup) of the berry compote for garnishing. Spoon the remainder into the pudding basin cavity to come just below the top of the basin. Arrange the reserved three slices of bread on top of the berries, trimming to fit. Fold the plastic wrap over the pudding.

Place a plate on top of the pudding, making sure it sits inside the basin. Place a heavy weight on top to compress the pudding, and refrigerate overnight.

To serve: Unwrap the pudding and turn out onto a platter. Pour over the reserved berry compote and serve with crème anglaise.

Note: The pudding must be made at least a day or up to 3 days in advance of serving.

Nothing beats the smell and taste of freshly baked mince pies as they come out of the oven. Our fruit mince is adapted from a collation of our family recipes and contains a sticky mixture of fruit, apples and warming spices all bound with a generous glug of brandy.

We easily gain a few extra kilos over this period!

CHRISTMAS MINCE PIES

Makes 24 mince pies • **Preparation time** Fruit Mince: soaking fruit up to 2 months; Pastry: 50 minutes plus 1 hour chilling time • **Cooking time** 25 minutes

For the fruit mince: Mix together the raisins, sultanas and currants in a food processor. Pulse the dried fruit mix until coarsely chopped.

Transfer the mixture into a large mixing bowl and add the rest of the ingredients. Mix with a wooden spoon until all incorporated.

Place in a sealed container and store in the fridge until needed.

For the pastry: Sift the flours and icing sugar into a bowl. Use an electric mixer fitted with a paddle attachment, add the butter and mix until it resembles fine breadcrumbs.

Mix the egg yolks and the iced water and pour into the flour and butter, then mix at low speed until just combined.

Remove from the bowl, press into a disc and wrap in plastic wrap. Rest for at least 1 hour in the fridge before using.

Preheat the oven to 180°C (350°F). Lightly grease two 12-hole 80 ml (2½ fl oz/⅓ cup) muffin tins.

To assemble: On a lightly floured surface, roll out the pastry to 3 mm (⅛ inch) thickness. Using an 8 cm (3¼ inch) round pastry cutter, cut out 24 rounds and place into the prepared pans. Spoon 2–3 teaspoons of fruit mince into each.

Re-knead the scraps and chill before rolling again. Roll and cut out lids to desired shapes, such as stars and rounds, and sprinkle with sugar. Bake for 20–25 minutes until golden. Leave to cool in the pans.

Note: It is best to make the filling up to 2 months in advance to let the flavours develop. The pastry can also be made up to 4 days ahead or frozen for up to 1 month.

FRUIT MINCE

470 g (1 lb ½ oz/2¾ cups) raisins
460 g (1 lb ¼ oz/2⅔ cups) sultanas (golden raisins)
450 g (1 lb) currants
2 apples, peeled, cored and grated
310 g (11 oz/1⅓ cups, lightly packed) light brown sugar
150 g (5½ oz) butter, melted
1 teaspoon ground cinnamon
½ teaspoon freshly grated nutmeg
½ teaspoon ground cloves
finely grated zest and juice of 1 lemon
finely grated zest and juice of 1 orange
200 ml (7 fl oz) brandy

PASTRY

350 g (12 oz/2⅓ cups) plain (all-purpose) flour
110 g (3¾ oz/¾ cup) self-raising flour
90 g (3¼ oz/¾ cup) icing (confectioners') sugar
240 g (8½ oz) cold butter, diced
2 egg yolks, at room temperature
50 ml (1¾ fl oz) iced water

caster, rapadura (panela) or raw sugar, to sprinkle

A rich fruitcake is hard to beat for Christmas. Though our recipe may look complicated at first glance it is, in fact, very easy if you prepare and weigh all the ingredients and line the tin before you start.

143

CHRISTMAS CAKE

215 g (7½ oz/1¼ cups) sultanas (golden raisins)

195 g (6¾ oz/1⅓ cups) currants

150 g (5½ oz/⅔ cup) pitted prunes, halved

110 g (3¾ oz/⅔ cup) mixed peel (mixed candied citrus peel), home-made or best quality store-bought

120 g (4¼ oz/⅔ cup) raisins

1 apple, peeled, cored and grated

4 tablespoons marmalade

60 ml (2 fl oz/¼ cup) brandy

finely grated zest and juice of 1 lemon

finely grated zest and juice of 1 orange

150 g (5½ oz/1 cup) plain (all-purpose) flour

1 teaspoon ground cinnamon

1 teaspoon mixed spice

½ teaspoon salt

125 g (4½ oz) butter, softened

125 g (4½ oz/⅔ cup, lightly packed) light brown sugar

90 g (3¼ oz/¼ cup) golden syrup (light treacle)

3 eggs, at room temperature

100 g (3½ oz/1 cup) almond meal

ICING

500 g (1 lb 2 oz) ready-made marzipan

3 tablespoons apricot jam, heated and sieved

500 g (1 lb 2 oz) ready-made fondant

1 egg white

Makes one 25 cm round cake • **Preparation time** 30 minutes plus overnight soaking time for fruit and 30 minutes icing the cake • **Cooking time** 1 hour 30 minutes

In a large ceramic or glass bowl, combine the sultanas, currants, prunes, mixed peel, raisins, apple, marmalade, brandy, citrus zests and juices and soak overnight at room temperature.

Preheat the oven to 160°C (315°F). Lightly grease and line the base and side of a 25 cm (10 inch) round cake tin with several layers of baking paper.

Sift the flour, cinnamon, mixed spice and salt together.

Using an electric mixer with a beater attachment, cream the butter and sugar until pale and creamy. Mix in the golden syrup, then add the eggs, one at a time, beating well after each addition. Gently fold in the sifted ingredients and almond meal. Finally, fold in the fruit mixture.

Spoon the mixture into the lined tin and smooth the surface. Bake for approximately 1½ hours, or until a skewer inserted into the middle of the cake comes out clean.

Cool completely in the tin. Remove the cake from the tin, and wrap in baking paper and foil. Keep in a cool dark place until ready to eat.

To ice the cake, trim the top to ensure it is flat, and patch any holes on the cake with marzipan. Knead the marzipan until smooth, roll out to a 6 mm (¼ inch) thickness, and cut out a 25 cm (10 inch) circle. Brush the top of the cake with the warmed and sieved apricot jam. Place the marzipan on top of the cake, pressing down until smooth. Knead and roll out the fondant to the same thickness and cut out another 25 cm (10 inch) circle. Lightly brush the marzipan with the lightly beaten egg white and finish off with the fondant layer.

Decorate as desired.

Notes: This cake can be made 3–4 months ahead and left un-iced. Once iced, store in an airtight container for up to 1 month.

Making hot cross buns is not difficult, all you need is some time up your sleeve. Our buns are laden with apricots and with sultanas that have been soaked in Earl Grey tea, adding a lovely fragrance and flavour, then spruced up with a sugar glaze to give them a high-gloss finish.

We promise you will never buy the shop versions again.

HOT CROSS BUNS

Makes 18 buns • **Preparation time** 45 minutes plus 30 minutes soaking time for sultanas plus 45 minutes first proving time for dough and 45 minutes second proving • **Cooking time** 35 minutes

Soak the sultanas in the tea for 30 minutes, then drain thoroughly.

Preheat the oven to 180°C (350°F). Line a large baking tray with baking paper.

In a medium saucepan, warm the skim milk and 200 ml (7 fl oz) water to 30°C (85°F) on a thermometer, then remove from the heat. Add the yeast, sugar and egg and stir until the yeast is dissolved. Set aside.

Sift together the flour, mixed spice and salt into the bowl of an electric stand mixer fitted with a dough hook attachment. Add the softened butter and the yeast mix. Knead on low speed until just incorporated. Turn the speed to medium and mix for 8 minutes. Add the fruit and knead until all the fruit is evenly distributed through the dough, approximately 1–2 minutes.

Remove the dough to a lightly floured surface and knead for 1 minute. Form a ball, and place the dough into a large, lightly greased bowl, then cover with plastic wrap and leave in a warm place to prove for approximately 45 minutes or until doubled in size.

Divide into 18 equal pieces and roll into taut balls. Place on the prepared tray, allowing room for spreading. Cover loosely with plastic wrap, leave in a warm place and prove for 45 minutes until doubled in size.

For the piping paste: In a small bowl, mix the flour with the sugar and 60 ml (2 fl oz/¼ cup) water until smooth. Fill a piping (icing) bag fitted with a 5–6 mm (¼ inch) plain nozzle, and pipe crosses on top of the buns.

Bake for 20–25 minutes until golden brown and the buns sound hollow when tapped on the base.

To glaze: In a small saucepan, dissolve the sugar and 50 ml (1¾ fl oz) water and bring to the boil. Brush this glaze over the buns.

Best eaten on the day or can be toasted up to 2 days later. Eat with lashings of butter!

200 g (7 oz) sultanas (golden raisins)
250 ml (9 fl oz/1 cup) Earl Grey tea, strong and hot
250 ml (9 fl oz/1 cup) skim milk
10 g (¼ oz/2 teaspoons) dried yeast
110 g (3¾ oz/½ cup) caster (superfine) sugar
1 egg, at room temperature, lightly beaten
860 g (1 lb 14½ oz/5¾ cups) strong (bread) flour
2 tablespoons mixed spice
1 teaspoon salt
85 g (3 oz) butter, softened
130 g (4½ oz/¾ cup) dried apricots, diced

PIPING PASTE

4 tablespoons plain (all-purpose) flour
1 tablespoon caster (superfine) sugar

GLAZE

110 g (3¾ oz/½ cup) caster (superfine) sugar

butter, to serve

Bite into a slice of our panforte and you may be surprised at how chewy it is. Mixing the fruits, spices, nuts, cocoa powder and flour with a syrup made from sugar and honey gives the cake an almost candy-like texture. Panforte stores well, so you can hide it away and cut off small pieces any time of the year when you have a sweet craving.

PANFORTE

3 rice paper sheets

350 g (12 oz/2⅓ cups) plain (all-purpose) flour

30 g (1 oz/¼ cup) dark cocoa powder

1½ teaspoons ground cinnamon

1½ teaspoons freshly ground black pepper

1 teaspoon ground ginger

½ teaspoon ground cloves

½ teaspoon freshly grated nutmeg

375 g (13 oz/2⅓ cups) blanched almonds, lightly toasted

375 g (13 oz/2⅔ cups) skinned hazelnuts, lightly toasted

290 g (10¼ oz/1⅔ cup) raisins

185 g (6½ oz/1 cup) whole dried figs, quartered

180 g (6¼ oz/1¼ cups) currants

200 g (7 oz/1¼ cups) dried apricots, diced

205 g (7¼ oz/1 cup) prunes, pitted and halved

125 g (4½ oz) cedro, or mixed peel, finely diced

370 g (13 oz/1⅔ cups) caster (superfine) sugar

260 g (9¼ oz/¾ cup) honey

Makes one 20 x 30 cm cake • **Preparation time** 40 minutes • **Cooking time** 1 hour

Preheat the oven to 150°C (300°F). Lightly grease and line a 20 x 30 cm (8 x 12 inch) slab tin with the rice paper sheets, trimming to fit.

In a large bowl, sift together the flour, cocoa powder and spices. Add in all the nuts and dried fruit and mix well.

In a heavy-based medium saucepan, combine the sugar and honey, and bring slowly to the boil. Cook until the mixture reaches the soft ball stage, at 116°C (241°F) measured using a sugar thermometer, about 15 minutes. Be cautious as you pour the syrup into the fruit and nut mix. Very carefully and quickly stir with a wooden spoon until combined and evenly coated – this is not an easy job.

Press evenly into the prepared tin. Bake for approximately 45 minutes or until the top of the panforte is matt in appearance. Cool in the tin.

Turn out onto a chopping board and carefully cut into pieces with a serrated knife using a sawing motion.

Note: Panforte can be made in advance and kept at room temperature in an airtight container for up to 2 months – but we suspect yours will be eaten long before that!

This recipe came from one of our biggest fans – Aunty Sue Coyle. You will enjoy the contrasts of a crispy exterior, soft chewy centre, tart dried cranberries and the bittersweet flavour of dark chocolate.

COCONUT AND CRANBERRY MACAROONS

Makes 12 • **Preparation time** 20 minutes • **Cooking time** 30 minutes

Preheat the oven to 180°C (350°F). Line a baking tray with baking paper.

Combine the caster sugar, glucose and egg whites in a medium saucepan. Cook over low heat until the mixture reaches 60°C (140°F) on a sugar thermometer, stirring constantly.

Remove the saucepan from the heat, then add the thread and desiccated coconuts, the flour and cranberries. Mix until just incorporated.

Divide the mixture into 12 equal portions and shape as desired. Bake for approximately 12–15 minutes until a light golden brown.

Leave to cool completely on the tray. At this stage you can dip in melted dark chocolate or dust with icing sugar, if desired.

Notes: Store in an airtight container. These keep for up to 1 week.

220 g (7¾ oz/1 cup) caster (superfine) sugar

20 g (¾ oz) liquid glucose

3 egg whites, at room temperature

130 g (4½ oz/2 cups) thread (shredded) coconut

135 g (4¾ oz/1½ cups) desiccated coconut

10 g (¼ oz/2 teaspoons) gluten-free plain flour

75 g (2¾ oz/½ cup) dried cranberries, chopped

melted dark chocolate, to dip (optional)

icing (confectioners') sugar, to dust (optional)

CHAPTER №7

CONFECTIONERY

There is no better gift than something
that is made using your own hands and
given with your heart. And while making
confectionery from scratch may seem
intimidating, it's actually pretty easy.
When it all comes together, it's magic!

The ultimate Rocky Road, this recipe uses marshmallows, rose-flavoured Turkish delight, pistachio nuts, toasted macadamias, cranberries, freeze-dried raspberries and the best quality dark chocolate.

DARK CHOCOLATE ROCKY ROAD

Makes about 24 pieces • **Preparation time** 20 minutes plus overnight setting time • **Cooking time** 30 minutes

Lightly grease and line the base and sides of a 20 x 30 x 4 cm (8 x 12 x 1½ inch) slab tin with baking paper, extending the paper 2 cm (¾ inch) over the sides.

In a large bowl combine the marshmallows, cranberries, pistachios, macadamias and the Turkish delight.

To temper the dark chocolate: Place 1 kg (2 lb 4 oz) of the chocolate in a heatproof bowl over a saucepan of simmering water, and make sure the base of the bowl does not touch the water. Melt the chocolate, stirring constantly until it reaches 50°C (122°F) using a sugar thermometer. Take the bowl off the saucepan, add the remaining chocolate and combine. Keep stirring the chocolate until you get to 29°C (84°F) using the sugar thermometer.

Then reheat the chocolate over the saucepan of simmering water at a low heat to its using temperature of 32°C (90°F). When working with chocolate, make sure you keep it at using temperature or you run the risk of losing the chocolate temper.

Add the tempered chocolate to the marshmallow and cranberry mixture, and mix well to coat. Spoon the mixture into the prepared tin and press down with a spatula to level. Sprinkle with freeze-dried raspberries, if using, and leave overnight to set.

Cut into bars or squares.

Notes: We use a dark couverture chocolate for our Rocky Road, which needs to be tempered. You can use compound chocolate from the supermarket, which is easier to use as it doesn't need tempering, but it is not as special.

Store in a cool dry place in an airtight container for up to 2 weeks.

3 x 125 g (4½ oz) packets pink and white marshmallows

120 g (4¼ oz/¾ cup) sweetened dried cranberries

90 g (3¼ oz/⅔ cup) pistachio kernels

265 g (9¼ oz/1⅔ cups) macadamia nuts, toasted

500 g (1 lb 2 oz) rose-flavoured Turkish delight, halved

1.5 kg (3 lb 5 oz) dark chocolate, chopped

30 g (1 oz/½ cup) freeze-dried raspberries (optional)

THE COOK AND BAKER

This is our updated version of a classic sweet. Using coconut oil and coconut cream will make this a definite prize winner at the school fete. Our apprentice Lizzy from Lancashire is our coconut ice queen!

RASPBERRY COCONUT ICE

1 kg (2 lb 4 oz/8 cups) icing (confectioners') sugar, sifted

495 g (1 lb 1½ oz/5½ cups) desiccated coconut

4 egg whites, at room temperature

250 ml (9 fl oz/1 cup) coconut oil, melted (not hot)

100 ml (3½ fl oz) coconut cream (not low fat)

2 teaspoons natural vanilla extract

2 teaspoons sea salt, crushed

pink food colouring

20 g (¾ oz) freeze-dried raspberries, crushed

Makes about 24 pieces • **Preparation time** 30 minutes plus 3 hours 15 minutes chilling time • **Cooking time** nil

Lightly grease and line the base and sides of a 20 x 30 x 4 cm (8 x 12 x 1½ inch) slab tin with baking paper.

Sift the icing sugar into a large bowl and mix in the desiccated coconut.

In another bowl, use a whisk to combine the egg whites, coconut oil and cream, vanilla and salt. Add the wet ingredients to the coconut and icing sugar, and with your hands mix until well combined.

Divide the mixture in half and add pink food colouring and half the freeze-dried raspberries to one portion, then knead the food colouring through until the colour is even.

Press the white mixture evenly over the base of the prepared tin and smooth the surface with your hand. Set in the fridge for 10–15 minutes before topping with the pink portion.

Sprinkle with the remaining crushed raspberries and lightly press into the mixture. Refrigerate for 2–3 hours or until firm.

Cut into bars or squares.

Note: Store in the fridge in an airtight container for up to 2 weeks.

Beware: your new salty-sweet addiction is going to get you in a whole lot of trouble!

It is vital that you use a sugar thermometer and watch it very carefully. If the temperature rises above 119°C (246°F), the result will be a hard chewy candy. If it doesn't reach that temperature, the caramel will be soft and pale.

SALTED CARAMELS

Makes about 40 pieces • **Preparation time** 20 minutes plus wrapping • **Cooking time** 30 minutes

Lightly grease and line the base and sides of a 20 x 30 x 4 cm (8 x 12 x 1½ inch) slab tin with a piece of baking paper.

In a medium saucepan, combine the cream, milk, caster and brown sugars, butter, glucose, sea salt flakes and 90 ml (3 fl oz) of water. Place over medium–high heat and cook, whisking constantly, until the mixture reaches 119°C (245°F) measured using a sugar thermometer, for about 25–30 minutes.

Once the caramel reaches 119°C (245°F), remove from the heat and pour into the prepared tray, making sure to scrape any caramel from the sides of the tin. Sprinkle sparingly with some extra sea salt and leave to cool completely.

Cut into 5 x 3 cm (2 x 1¼ inch) rectangles, wrap well in waxed paper or thick cellophane and twist at both ends.

Note: Store in an airtight container for up to 10 days.

750 ml (26 fl oz/3 cups) thin (pouring) cream
750 ml (26 fl oz/3 cups) milk
880 g (1 lb 15½ oz/4 cups) caster (superfine) sugar
470 g (1 lb ½ oz/2½ cups, lightly packed) light brown sugar
60 g (2¼ oz) unsalted butter
300 g (10½ oz/1 cup) liquid glucose
1 teaspoon sea salt flakes, plus extra, for sprinkling

*What an irresistible sugar hit! Caramel-coated clusters of popcorn —
light, crispy, sweet, salty and insane. It's also great with the addition of
salted peanuts or cashews. Once you start, you won't be able to stop.*

CARAMEL POPCORN

10 cups popped popcorn

470 g (1 lb ½ oz/2½ cups, lightly
packed) light brown sugar

450 g (1 lb) salted butter, chopped

300 g (10½ oz/1 cup) liquid glucose

1 teaspoon natural vanilla extract

1 teaspoon bicarbonate of soda
(baking soda)

½ teaspoon salt

Makes approximately 10 cups • **Preparation time** 20 minutes • **Cooking
time** 20 minutes

Preheat the oven to 180°C (350°F). Line two large baking trays with
baking paper.

Divide the popcorn between the baking trays. In a medium saucepan,
combine the sugar, butter and glucose. Cook over medium heat, stirring
constantly, until the mixture reaches 118°C (244°F) on a sugar thermometer.

Remove the saucepan from the heat and stir in the vanilla,
bicarbonate of soda and the salt. Pour the caramel over the popcorn,
and carefully stir to coat the popcorn evenly.

Place the trays in the oven and cook for 8 minutes, then remove the
trays and stir the popcorn to ensure the caramel is evenly distributed.
Leave to cool.

When completely cooled, break into chunks of caramel popcorn and
store in an airtight container.

Note: Caramel popcorn will last for up to 1 week in an airtight container.

CONFECTIONERY

It's all about the peanuts and sugar. This recipe is a world apart from the store-bought variety. And everyone loves peanut brittle — it's the perfect sweet treat for your own indulgence or to share.

PEANUT BRITTLE

Makes approximately 1 kg (2 lb 4 oz) slab of brittle • **Preparation time** 10 minutes • **Cooking time** 20 minutes

Lightly grease and line a large baking tray with baking paper.

In a large heavy-based saucepan, combine the sugar, 185 ml (6 fl oz/¾ cup) water and the glucose. Cook the sugar until it is amber in colour, approximately 15–20 minutes.

Add the peanuts and stir gently until coated. Quickly mix in the butter, vanilla and bicarbonate of soda, and stir gently.

Pour the mixture onto the prepared tray and spread with the back of a spatula to a 1 cm (½ inch) thickness. Leave to cool completely before snapping into pieces.

Note: Store in an airtight container for up to 1 week.

550 g (1 lb 4 oz/2½ cups) caster (superfine) sugar
150 g (5½ oz/½ cup) liquid glucose
450 g (1 lb) whole blanched peanuts
30 g (1 oz) butter
1 teaspoon natural vanilla extract
½ teaspoon bicarbonate of soda (baking soda)

This charmingly old-fashioned recipe belongs to Tass's dear Aunty Erena. He has fond memories of her serving these marshmallows as part of Devonshire tea at her homestead.

VANILLA AND TOASTED COCONUT MARSHMALLOW

495 g (1 lb 1½ oz/2¼ cups) caster (superfine) sugar

450 g (1 lb/1½ cups) liquid glucose

24 g (1 oz) gelatine leaves/sheets or 7 teaspoons powdered gelatine

1 teaspoon natural vanilla extract

3 egg whites, at room temperature

½ teaspoon salt

cooking oil spray

195 g (6¾ oz/3 cups) thread (shredded) coconut, lightly toasted, to coat

Makes about 24 pieces • **Preparation time** 30 minutes plus 5–6 hours or overnight to set • **Cooking time** 10 minutes

Lightly grease and line the base and sides of a 20 x 30 x 4 cm (8 x 12 x 1½ inch) slab tin with baking paper.

In a heavy-based saucepan, place the sugar, glucose and 185 ml (6 fl oz/¾ cup) water and heat, without stirring, to 127°C (261°F) measured using a sugar thermometer, for approximately 10 minutes.

While the syrup is coming up to temperature, soak the gelatine sheets in cold water for 5 minutes or until soft and hydrated, then drain. If using powdered gelatine: In a small bowl, sprinkle the gelatine over the surface of 80 ml (2½ fl oz/⅓ cup) water, and set aside to dissolve.

When the syrup reaches 127°C, take off the heat, add the gelatine and vanilla and whisk until no lumps remain.

Using an electric mixer fitted with a whisk attachment, whisk the egg whites and salt until light and fluffy. Stop the mixer and pour the syrup over the egg whites, gradually turn the speed to high and continue whisking until the mixture thickens, becomes glossy and has cooled a little.

Pour the mixture into the prepared tin and spread evenly. Lightly spray the top of the mixture with oil spray, then place a piece of baking paper on top, and use your hand to level and press the mixture into the corners.

Let cool until set, approximately 5–6 hours or overnight. Remove the baking paper from the top, and sprinkle with some of the toasted coconut. Turn out onto a work surface, remove the other piece of baking paper and cut into 5 x 5 cm (2 x 2 inch) squares, then coat the marshmallow in the remaining toasted coconut.

Note: Store in an airtight container for up to 1 week.

Quick hide it, Cherie's coming!

Fudge was one of the first sweets Cherie made as a young girl. Time and time again she made the overcooked, sugary fudge that only a child would love. Now she has perfected a recipe that is soft, creamy and decadent.

CARAMEL FUDGE

Makes about 24 pieces • **Preparation time** 20 minutes plus setting time • **Cooking time** 20 minutes

Lightly grease and line the base and sides of a 20 x 30 x 4 cm (8 x 12 x 1½ inch) slab tin with baking paper.

In a heavy-based saucepan combine the sugar, condensed milk, butter, golden syrup, 80 ml (2½ fl oz/⅓ cup) water, vanilla and salt. Stir over low heat continuously for about 5 minutes or until the sugar has dissolved and the mixture looks even.

Increase the heat to a simmer, stirring constantly, and cook until it reaches 106°C (223°F) on a sugar thermometer, for approximately 10–15 minutes. Remove from the heat, add the chocolate and stir in gently, being careful to not overwork it.

Pour into the prepared tin and leave to set at room temperature.

Cut into 5 x 5 cm (2 x 2 inch) pieces.

Note: Store in an airtight container for up to 2 weeks.

415 g (14¾ oz/2¼ cups, lightly packed) light brown sugar

2 x 395 g (14 oz) tins condensed milk

160 g (5¾ oz) unsalted butter, chopped

90 g (3¼ oz/¼ cup) golden syrup (light treacle)

2 teaspoons natural vanilla extract

2 teaspoons sea salt

360 g (12¾ oz) white chocolate

Nougat may seem intimidating, but it's really just sugar syrup that has been whipped into egg whites. Even though this recipe is quite labour-intensive, you will be rewarded with the most fabulous nougat.

Thank you Jessica Pedemont, the chocolate artisan, for this recipe. You have taught us many skills in the world of confectionery.

CHOCOLATE, ALMOND AND SOUR CHERRY NOUGAT

5 rice paper sheets

BATCH 1
180 g (6¼ oz) caster (superfine) sugar
300 g (10½ oz/1 cup) liquid glucose

BATCH 2
330 g (11½ cups) caster (superfine) sugar
300 g (10½ oz/1 cup) liquid glucose

100 g (3½ oz) egg whites (3 large eggs)
35 g (1¼ oz) caster (superfine) sugar
½ teaspoon sea salt
115 g (4 oz/⅓ cup) honey
1 teaspoon natural vanilla extract
500 g (1 lb 2 oz) blanched almonds, lightly toasted
200 g (7 oz/1⅓ cups) chopped dark chocolate
150 g (5½ oz) dried sour cherries

Makes 12 bars • **Preparation time** 30 minutes • **Cooking time** 35 minutes

Lightly grease a 20 x 30 x 4 cm (8 x 12 x 1½ inch) slab tin. Line the tin with a single layer of rice paper.

In a medium saucepan, combine the first batch of sugar and glucose with 80 ml (2½ fl oz/⅓ cup) water, place over medium–high heat and cook until the mixture reaches 122°C (252°F) on a sugar thermometer, for approximately 10–15 minutes.

At the same time in another saucepan combine the second batch of sugar and glucose with 125 ml (4 fl oz/½ cup) water and cook until it reaches 145°C (293°F) on a sugar thermometer, for approximately 15–20 minutes.

In the bowl of an electric mixer fitted with a whisk attachment, whisk the egg whites until they reach the soft peak stage, then add the remaining 35 g (1¼ oz) sugar and the salt, followed by the first batch of liquid sugar, then add the second batch.

Once all combined, add the honey and vanilla. Whisk for 5 minutes and while the mixture is still warm, take off the electric mixer and stir in the almonds, chocolate and sour cherries.

Pour into the prepared tin and level out with a palette knife. Cover the top with rice paper and set aside to cool.

Cut into twelve 5 x 10 cm (2 x 4 inch) bars or pieces.

Notes: Store in an airtight container. Nougat will keep well for up to 1 month.

CONFECTIONERY

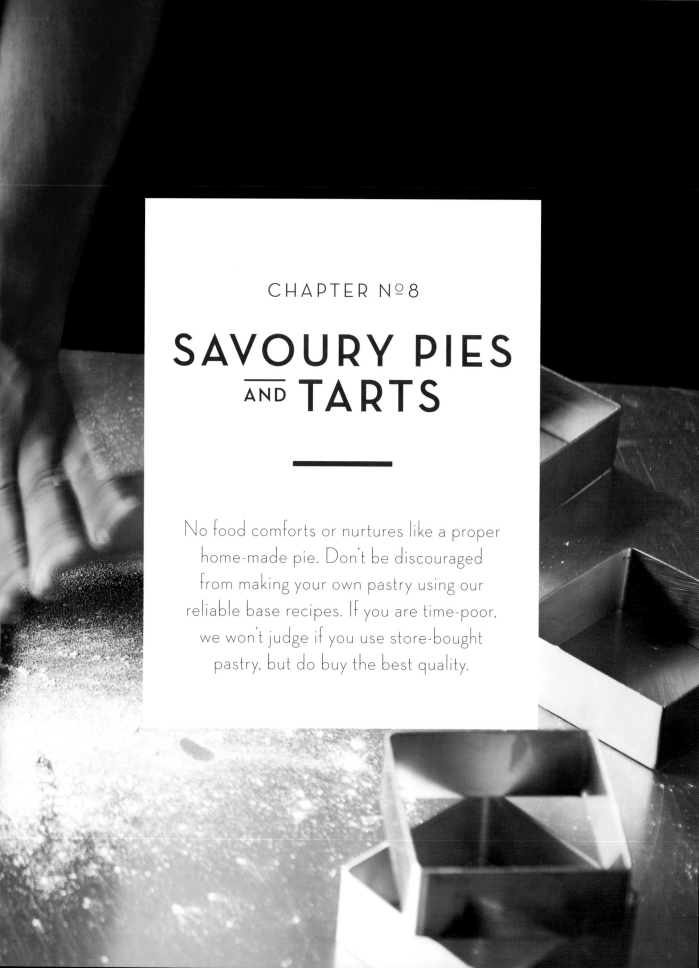

CHAPTER № 8

SAVOURY PIES AND TARTS

No food comforts or nurtures like a proper home-made pie. Don't be discouraged from making your own pastry using our reliable base recipes. If you are time-poor, we won't judge if you use store-bought pastry, but do buy the best quality.

This comforting pie is mild and creamy, packed with tender chicken, leeks and mushrooms, and is great for a family get-together. Served with potato mash, garden salad or steamed greens, this makes for quick and easy entertaining.

CHICKEN, MUSHROOM AND TARRAGON PIE

Serves 6–8 • **Makes** one 25 x 25 x 8 cm pie • **Preparation time** 45 minutes plus cooling time and 30 minutes chilling time for dough • **Cooking time** 1 hour 30 minutes

In a large saucepan, heat the oil over medium–high heat. Add the onion, leek and mushrooms and cook for 2 minutes.

Add the diced chicken thigh and stock and bring to the boil. Lower the heat and simmer gently for 40–45 minutes or until the chicken is cooked through and tender.

Make a slurry with the cornflour and 80 ml (2½ fl oz/⅓ cup) water, and pour enough of this mix into the chicken to thicken. Simmer for a further 10 minutes, then take off the heat and add the cream, chopped tarragon and season well with salt and pepper. Cool completely before using.

Preheat the oven to 180°C (350°F). Lightly grease a 25 x 25 x 8 cm (10 x 10 x 3¼ inch) pie dish.

To assemble the pie: On a lightly floured surface, roll the pie top to 4 mm (¼ inch) thick, then rest in the fridge for 30 minutes.

Fill the pie dish almost to the top with the cold pie filling and cover with the pie top. Trim the pastry overhang and fold over the edges. If desired, score the pastry with a sharp knife in a fanlike pattern such as shown in the photograph opposite. Glaze the top of the pie with the egg wash.

Bake for 25–30 minutes until the pastry is cooked and golden brown.

Notes: This pie will keep for 2–3 days in the fridge. The pie filling can be made 3 days prior to using and any left-over filling can be frozen for up to 1 month. If time-poor, use good quality store-bought puff pastry.

2 tablespoons vegetable oil

2 brown onions, diced

1 leek, pale part only, thinly sliced into 1 cm (½ inch) rounds

250 g (9 oz) button mushrooms, quartered

1 kg (2 lb 4 oz) boneless, skinless chicken thighs, diced

250 ml (9 fl oz/1 cup) chicken stock

2 tablespoons cornflour (cornstarch)

200 ml (7 fl oz) thin (pouring) cream, to finish

½ bunch (1 tablespoon) tarragon leaves, picked and chopped

salt and pepper

½ quantity Pie Top (see page 219)

egg wash (beat 1 egg yolk with 2 tablespoons thin (pouring) cream)

The beauty of a frittata is that it feeds a crowd and keeps well. It's also a quick and easy, gluten-free option for breakfast or a light lunch. Serve with a simple salad. You can vary the filling by using other roasted vegetables or different cheeses.

SWEET POTATO, ROAST CAPSICUM AND THYME FRITTATA

2 large sweet potatoes, peeled and cut into 4 cm (1½ inch) cubes

2 red capsicums (peppers), seeded and thickly sliced

olive oil, to drizzle

100 g (3½ oz/2¼ cups) baby English spinach leaves

25 g (1 oz/¼ cup) grated parmesan

1 tablespoon thyme leaves, chopped

salt and pepper

1½ quantities Custard Filling (Savoury) (see page 221)

Serves 4–6 • **Makes** one 30 cm frittata • **Preparation time** 25 minutes plus cooling time • **Cooking time** 1 hour 10 minutes

Preheat the oven to 180°C (350°F). Line two baking tins with baking paper.

Spread the sweet potato and capsicum separately in the tins. Drizzle with olive oil, then bake for 20–25 minutes until cooked. Set aside to cool.

Lightly grease a 30 cm (12 inch) ovenproof dish. Place the spinach, roasted sweet potato and capsicum in the dish, sprinkle with the parmesan and thyme, season with salt and pepper, and pour over enough custard to completely cover the vegetables.

Bake for 40–45 minutes until the filling has just set and is golden brown. If the top browns too quickly, cover with foil and keep cooking until the custard is set.

This is delicious served hot or at room temperature.

The delicious partnership of roasted pumpkin, ricotta and caramelised onion makes this a great summer tart to take to a picnic in the park. It will only take moments to assemble once you have made the pizza dough and filling.

RUSTIC PUMPKIN, RICOTTA AND CARAMELISED ONION TART

Serves 8 • **Makes** one 30 cm (12 inch) tart • **Preparation time** 30 minutes plus cooling time • **Cooking time** 1 hour 10 minutes

Preheat the oven to 180°C (350°F). Line a baking tin with baking paper. Toss in the pumpkin cubes with enough oil to lightly coat. Roast for 20 minutes or until tender. Remove from the oven and leave to cool.

Sauté the spinach in a frying pan over high heat for 1–2 minutes until wilted, leave to cool, then use your hands to squeeze dry.

In a large bowl combine the ricotta, parmesan, eggs and salt and pepper. Fold through the pumpkin, spinach and caramelised onions.

Line a baking tray with baking paper. On a lightly floured surface, roll out the pizza dough to 40 cm (16 inches) round and 5 mm (¼ inch) thick.

Transfer the rolled dough to the prepared tray. Spread the ricotta mix over the pizza dough leaving a 5 cm (2 inch) border. Gather the edge of the dough and drape back over the filling to create a ruffled look.

Bake for 40–45 minutes or until the crust is golden brown. Drizzle with olive oil and serve.

This is delicious served hot or at room temperature.

750 g (1 lb 10 oz/5 cups) seeded, peeled and chopped into 3 cm (1¼ inch) pieces uncooked pumpkin
olive oil, to coat and drizzle
250 g (9 oz/6¼ cups) English spinach
1 kg (2 lb 4 oz/4⅓ cups) fresh ricotta cheese
25 g (1 oz/¼ cup) grated parmesan
2 eggs, at room temperature, lightly beaten
salt and pepper
125 g (4½ oz/½ cup) Caramelised Onion (see page 229)
1 quantity Pizza Dough (see page 220)

THE COOK AND BAKER

One of the best things in life is the simple pleasure that comes from fresh ingredients. The ratatouille for our pie is a fine example and sings with summer vegetables. Ratatouille can also be enjoyed on its own as a simple meal.

RATATOUILLE PIE

ROAST VEGETABLES

2 eggplants (aubergines), diced

2 red capsicums (peppers), seeded and diced

4 zucchini (courgettes), diced

120 ml (4 fl oz) tablespoons olive oil

salt and pepper

TOMATO SAUCE

2 tablespoons olive oil

2 red onions, diced

2 garlic cloves, chopped

2 x 400 g (14 oz) tins chopped tomatoes

2 tablespoons tomato paste (concentrated purée)

15 g (½ oz/¼ cup, firmly packed) chopped basil

salt and pepper

½ quantity Pie Top (see page 219)

1½ quantities Pie Base (see page 218)

egg wash (beat 1 egg yolk with 2 tablespoons thin (pouring) cream)

Serves 6 • **Makes** six 10 x 10 x 4 cm square pies • **Preparation time** 30 minutes plus cooling time and 30 minutes chilling time for pastry • **Cooking time** 1 hour 30 minutes

Preheat the oven to 180°C (350°F). Line three baking trays with baking paper.

To roast the vegetables: In a bowl, toss each vegetable separately with 2 tablespoons of oil and season well with salt and pepper. Place on the prepared trays. Roast for 15–20 minutes or until tender.

Meanwhile, make the tomato sauce. In a large saucepan, heat the oil over medium heat. Add the onion and garlic and cook for 5 minutes, or until soft.

Add the tomatoes and tomato paste, bring to the boil, then lower the heat to a simmer and cook for 30 minutes. Finish the sauce with the basil. Set aside.

Add the roasted vegetables to the tomato sauce and season well. Cool completely before using.

Reheat the oven to 180°C (350°F). Lightly grease six 10 x 10 x 4 cm (4 x 4 x 1½ inch) pie tins.

To assemble the pies: On a lightly floured surface, roll the pie base and the pie top to 4 mm (¼ inch) thick, then chill in the fridge for 30 minutes. Remove the pastries from the fridge and line the tins with the pie base allowing a 1 cm (½ inch) overhang.

Fill the pastry-lined tins almost to the top with the cold ratatouille. Brush the pastry edge with egg wash and cover with the pie top, pressing the edges together to seal. Trim the pastry overhang and glaze the top of the pies with egg wash.

Bake for 30–35 minutes until pastry is cooked and golden brown.

Note: The pie filling can be made 3 days prior to using and any left-over filling can be frozen for up to 1 month.

SAVOURY PIES AND TARTS

We love tarts and their versatility. The seasons play a vital role in selecting the fillings — so many variations and combinations of meat, fish, vegetables and herbs can be used. Use our pastry and custard filling as your base and let your culinary imagination run wild.

CAULIFLOWER AND CHEESE SAUCE TART

Serves 4–6 • **Makes** one 11 x 34 x 2.5 cm tart • **Preparation time** 40 minutes plus 30 minutes chilling time for pastry • **Cooking time** 1 hour 30 minutes

1 quantity Pie Base (see page 218)

½ cauliflower, cut into florets

250 ml (9 fl oz/1 cup) milk

25 g (1 oz) butter

35 g (1¼ oz/¼ cup) plain (all-purpose) flour

100 g (3½ oz/1 cup) grated cheddar cheese

salt and pepper

100 g (3½ oz/2¼ cups) baby English spinach leaves

1 tablespoon grated parmesan

1 quantity Custard Filling (Savoury) (see page 221)

Preheat the oven to 180°C (350°F). Lightly grease an 11 x 34 x 2.5 cm (4¼ x 13½ x 1 inch) fluted rectangular loose-based flan (tart) tin.

Remove the pie base pastry from the fridge, lightly dust your work surface with flour and roll out the pastry to fit the tin, approximately 3 mm (⅛ inch) in thickness. Line the tin with the pastry, leaving a slight overhang. Chill in the fridge for 30 minutes before trimming the edges.

To blind bake the pastry: Line the pastry shell with a piece of crumpled baking paper and pour in some baking beads or uncooked rice or dried beans. Bake for 15 minutes, then remove the paper and beans and return to the oven for another 5–10 minutes, until the pastry is dry and just turning golden. Cool a little.

For the cauliflower filling: Cook the cauliflower florets in a saucepan of boiling water for 3–4 minutes, until tender. Drain well. Heat the milk in a small saucepan over medium heat until just hot. Melt the butter in another saucepan over medium heat, stir in the flour and cook for 2 minutes, stirring. Gradually whisk in the hot milk and stir until it reaches simmering point. Simmer for at least 20 minutes before adding in the cheese. Stir in the cheddar cheese, and season well with salt and pepper.

Place the cauliflower in an oven dish, pour over the cheese sauce and bake at 180°C (350°F) for approximately 15–20 minutes until golden brown. Remove from the oven and cool.

To assemble the tart: Scatter the spinach into the tart shell, then nestle the cauliflower cheese among the spinach leaves and sprinkle with the parmesan. Pour in as much of the custard filling as you can without it spilling over the edge. Return to the oven and bake for a further 25–30 minutes until the egg custard has set and is golden brown.

Serve hot or at room temperature.

CHERRY TOMATO, GOAT'S CHEESE AND BASIL TART

Serves 4–6 • **Makes** one 11 x 34 x 2.5 cm tart • **Preparation time** 20 minutes plus 30 minutes chilling time for pastry • **Cooking time** 55 minutes

1 quantity Pie Base (see page 218)

100 g (3½ oz/2¼ cups) baby English spinach leaves

10 basil leaves

250 g (9 oz) cherry tomatoes

150 g (5½ oz/1¼ cups) crumbled goat's cheese

1 quantity Custard Filling (Savoury) (see page 221)

Preheat the oven to 180°C (350°F). Lightly grease an 11 x 34 x 2.5 cm (4¼ x 13½ x 1 inch) fluted rectangular loose-based flan (tart) tin.

Remove the pie base from the fridge, lightly dust your work surface with flour and roll out the pastry to fit the tin, approximately 3 mm (⅛ inch) in thickness. Line the tin with the pastry, leaving a slight overhang. Chill in the fridge for 30 minutes before trimming the edges. Blind bake (see page 180) for at least 20–25 minutes, until the pastry is dry and just turning golden. Cool a little.

To assemble the tart: Place the spinach and basil in the tart shell, then nestle the tomatoes among the baby spinach leaves. Dot with the goat's cheese and pour in as much of the custard filling as you can without it spilling over the edge. Return to the oven and bake for a further 25–30 minutes until the egg custard has set and is golden brown.

Serve hot or at room temperature.

BACON, EGG AND CHERRY TOMATO TART

Serves 4–6 • **Makes** one 11 x 34 x 2.5 cm tart • **Preparation time** 20 minutes plus 30 minutes chilling time for pastry • **Cooking time** 55 minutes

1 quantity Pie Base (see page 218)

4 bacon rashers, trimmed

250 g (9 oz) cherry tomatoes

1 quantity Custard Filling (Savoury) (see page 221)

Preheat the oven to 180°C (350°F). Lightly grease an 11 x 34 x 2.5 cm (4¼ x 13½ x 1 inch) fluted rectangular loose-based flan (tart) tin.

Remove the pie base from the fridge, lightly dust your work surface with flour and roll out the pastry to fit the tin, approximately 3 mm (⅛ inch) in thickness. Line the tin with the pastry, leaving a slight overhang. Chill in the fridge for 30 minutes before trimming the edges. Blind bake (see page 180) for at least 20–25 minutes, until the pastry is dry and just turning golden. Cool a little.

To assemble the tart: Arrange the bacon in the tart shell and dot with cherry tomatoes. Pour in as much of the custard filling as you can without it spilling over the edge. Return to the oven and bake for a further 25–30 minutes until the egg custard has set and is golden brown.

Serve hot or at room temperature.

ASPARAGUS, PEA, LEEK AND RICOTTA TART

1 quantity Pie Base (see page 218)

20 g (¾ oz) butter

1 leek, pale part only, thinly sliced

2 bunches asparagus

140 g (5 oz/1 cup) frozen peas, defrosted

150 g (5½ oz) fresh ricotta cheese

4 tablespoons grated parmesan

100 g (3½ oz/2¼ cups) baby English spinach leaves

1 quantity Custard Filling (Savoury) (see page 221)

Serves 4–6 • **Makes** one 11 x 34 x 2.5 cm tart • **Preparation time** 20 minutes plus 30 minutes chilling time for pastry • **Cooking time** 1 hour

Preheat the oven to 180°C (350°F). Lightly grease an 11 x 34 x 2.5 cm (4¼ x 13½ x 1 inch) fluted rectangular loose-based flan (tart) tin.

Remove the pie base from the fridge, lightly dust your work surface with flour and roll out the pastry to fit the tin, approximately 3 mm (⅛ inch) in thickness. Line the tin with the pastry, leaving a slight overhang. Chill in the fridge for 30 minutes before trimming the edges. Blind bake (see page 180) for at least 20–25 minutes, until the pastry is dry and just turning golden. Cool a little.

For the filling: Heat a small frying pan over medium heat. Melt the butter and sauté the leek for 3–4 minutes until softened. Trim the asparagus, cut the spears in half, and keep aside the tips for garnishing the top of tart. In a small bowl mix together the asparagus ends, peas, cooked leek, ricotta and 2 tablespoons of the grated parmesan.

To assemble the tart: Place the spinach in the tart shell, nestle the asparagus and pea mixture among the spinach. Garnish with the asparagus tips, sprinkle over the remaining parmesan. Pour in as much of the custard filling as you can without it spilling over the edge. Return to the oven and bake for a further 25–30 minutes until the egg custard has set and is golden brown.

Serve hot or at room temperature.

A proper beef pie with chunks of tender meat, rich gravy and masses of flavour, this is the perfect steak pie. It will warm your cockles on a cold winter's day.

BEEF AND ALE PIE

Makes twenty-four 7 cm party pies • **Preparation time** 40 minutes plus cooling time and 30 minutes chilling time for pastry • **Cooking time** 3 hours

In a large saucepan, heat 2 tablespoons of the oil over medium–high heat and add the beef in batches, removing them to a side plate when fully browned. Set aside.

Heat the remaining oil and add the onion, carrot and celery and cook for 5 minutes. Return the beef to the pan with the herbs, Vegemite and tomato paste and pour in enough stock to just cover the beef.

Bring to the boil then reduce to a simmer and cook for approximately 1½–2 hours or until the meat is just tender.

Add the ale and bring back to the boil. Mix the cornflour with enough water (about 120 ml/4 fl oz) to make a slurry, and pour enough of this mixture into the beef to thicken. Simmer for a further 10–15 minutes. Season well with salt and pepper. Cool completely before using.

Preheat the oven to 180°C (350°F). Lightly grease two 12-hole 80 ml (2½ fl oz/⅓ cup) muffin tins.

To assemble the pies: On a lightly floured surface, roll the pie base and the pie top to 4 mm (¼ inch) thick, then chill in the fridge for 30 minutes. Remove the pastries from the fridge. From the pie base, cut out twenty-four 8 cm (3¼ inch) circles. From the pie top, cut out twenty-four 7 cm (2¾ inch) circles.

Line the tins with the pie bases allowing a 5 mm (¼ inch) overhang.

Fill the pastry-lined tins almost to the top with the cold pie filling. Brush the pastry edge with egg wash and cover with the pie tops, pressing the edges together to seal. Trim the pastry overhang and glaze the top of the pies with the egg wash.

Bake for 25–30 minutes until the pastry is cooked and golden brown.

Note: The pie filling can be made 3 days prior to using and any left-over filling can be frozen for up to 1 month.

80 ml (2½ fl oz/⅓ cup) vegetable oil

1 kg (2 lb 4 oz) chuck steak, diced

2 brown onions, diced

2 carrots, diced

4 celery stalks, diced

1 tablespoon thyme, chopped

1 tablespoon rosemary, chopped

2 fresh bay leaves

1 tablespoon Vegemite or Marmite

1 tablespoon tomato paste (concentrated purée)

500 ml (17 fl oz/2 cups) beef or chicken stock

200 ml (7 fl oz) pale ale (beer)

4 tablespoons cornflour (cornstarch)

salt and pepper

1 quantity Pie Top (see page 219)

1½ quantities Pie Base (see page 218)

egg wash (beat 1 egg yolk with 2 tablespoons thin (pouring) cream)

THE COOK AND BAKER

An indelible memory of our school tuckshop days, when we thought the cellophane-bagged, soggy, under-baked pie, filled with gravy and minced (ground) meat was the best ever. How our tastebuds have matured! This is our version.

MINCE 'N' CHEESE PIE

2 brown onions, roughly diced

1 carrot, roughly diced

4 celery stalks, roughly diced

2 tablespoons vegetable oil

1 kg (2 lb 4 oz) minced (coarsely ground) beef

1 tablespoon thyme, chopped

2 fresh bay leaves

1 tablespoon Vegemite or Marmite

1 tablespoon tomato paste (concentrated purée)

1 litre (35 fl oz/4 cups) beef or chicken stock

4 tablespoons cornflour (cornstarch)

salt and pepper

125 g (4½ oz/1¼ cups) grated cheddar cheese

½ quantity Pie Top (see page 219)

1½ quantities Pie Base (see page 218)

egg wash (beat 1 egg yolk with 2 tablespoons thin (pouring) cream)

Makes six 10 x 10 x 4 cm pies • **Preparation time** 40 minutes plus cooling time and 30 minutes chilling time for pastry • **Cooking time** 1 hour 40 minutes

In a food processor, pulse the onion, carrot and celery until finely chopped.

In a large saucepan, heat the oil over medium–high heat. Add the chopped vegetables and cook for 5 minutes.

Increase the heat to high, then add the minced beef and cook until brown. Stir occasionally to prevent large lumps of meat forming.

Add the herbs, Vegemite, tomato paste and stock. Bring to the boil, lower the heat and simmer gently for 35–40 minutes.

Mix the cornflour with enough water (about 120 ml/4 fl oz) to make a slurry and pour enough of this mixture into the mince to thicken. Simmer for a further 10 minutes, then season well with salt and pepper. Cool completely before using.

Preheat the oven to 180°C (350°F). Lightly grease six 10 x 10 x 4 cm (4 x 4 x 1½ inch) square pie tins.

To assemble the pies: On a lightly floured surface, roll the pie base and the pie top to 4 mm (¼ inch) thick, then chill in the fridge for 30 minutes. Remove the pastries from the fridge and line the tins with the pie base allowing a 1 cm (½ inch) overhang.

Fill each pastry-lined tin almost to the top with the cooled mince, then add the grated cheddar. Brush the pastry edges with egg wash and cover with the pie tops, pressing the edges together to seal. Trim the pastry overhang and glaze the top of each pie with egg wash.

Bake for 30–35 minutes until the pastry is cooked and golden brown.

Note: The pie filling can be made 3 days prior to using and any left-over filling can be frozen for up to 1 month. If time-poor, use good quality store-bought pastry.

There are no rules for what makes a frittata. We often add smoked trout to our fennel, potato and caramelised onion frittata as a variation. Frittatas are an efficient way to use up your leftovers.

ROAST FENNEL, POTATO, CARAMELISED ONION AND OREGANO FRITTATA

Serves 4–6 • **Makes** one 20 x 30 x 6 cm frittata • **Preparation time** 25 minutes plus cooling time • **Cooking time** 1 hour 10 minutes

Preheat the oven to 180°C (350°F). Line two baking tins with baking paper and spread the fennel and potato separately into the tins. Drizzle with olive oil and bake for 20–25 minutes until cooked. Set aside to cool.

Lightly grease a 20 x 30 x 6 cm (8 x 12 x 2½ inch) ovenproof dish. Place the spinach, roasted fennel and potato, and caramelised onions in the dish, sprinkle with the parmesan and oregano, season with salt and pepper and pour over enough custard filling to completely cover the vegetables.

Bake for 40–45 minutes, until the filling has just set and is golden brown. If the top browns too quickly, cover with foil and keep cooking until the custard is set.

This is delicious served hot or at room temperature.

3 fennel bulbs, cut into wedges

3 large potatoes, peeled and cut into 3 cm (1¼ inch) cubes

olive oil, to drizzle

100 g (3½ oz/2¼ cups) baby English spinach leaves

60 g (2¼ oz/¼ cup) Caramelised Onion (see page 229)

25 g (1 oz/¼ cup) grated parmesan

1 tablespoon oregano leaves, chopped

salt and pepper

1½ quantities Custard Filling (Savoury) (see page 221)

This is the perfect big family meal. Poached blue eye cod and vegetables, bound in a béchamel sauce and topped with a rich, buttery, creamy mash, it is almost impossible to refuse a second helping of this nurturing pie.

BLUE EYE COD AND POTATO MASH PIE

Serves 6–8 • **Makes** one 30 cm pie • **Preparation time** 45 minutes • **Cooking time** 2 hours 15 minutes

POTATO MASH

1 kg (2 lb 4 oz) all-purpose potatoes, peeled and diced
100 ml (3½ fl oz) thin (pouring) cream
100 g (3½ oz) butter
salt and pepper
freshly grated nutmeg

PIE FILLING

1 kg (2 lb 4 oz) blue eye cod, filleted, boned and skinned
1 litre (35 fl oz/4 cups) milk
3 brown onions, sliced
2 fresh bay leaves
½ bunch thyme sprigs
8 black peppercorns
200 g (7 oz) butter
4 celery stalks, diced
1 celeriac, peeled and diced
2 carrots, diced
100 g (3½ oz/⅔ cup) plain (all-purpose) flour
salt and pepper

Preheat the oven to 180°C (350°F). Lightly grease a 30 cm (12 inch) oval ovenproof dish.

For the potato mash: Boil the potatoes for 12–15 minutes over medium–high heat, until soft. Drain and mash until smooth, then stir in the cream and butter and season well with salt, pepper and nutmeg. Cover and put aside to cool.

For the pie filling: Place the fish in a medium-deep roasting tin, add the milk, 1 of the sliced onions, the bay leaves, thyme and peppercorns and cover with foil. Bake for approximately 40–45 minutes until the fish is opaque and just cooked. Remove from the oven, and carefully remove the fish from the tin. Set aside.

Strain the milk through a sieve, discarding the onion, thyme, peppercorns and bay leaves. Keep this milk warm – it will be used to make the base sauce.

Melt the butter in a medium saucepan, and add the remaining onion, the celery, celeriac and carrot. Cover with a lid, and cook over low heat for 10–15 minutes, or until the vegetables are tender, particularly the carrots.

Stir in the flour and cook over medium heat for 5 minutes. Add the warm reserved milk. Bring slowly to the boil, stirring constantly, then lower the heat to a simmer and cook for a further 20 minutes. Season well.

Flake the fish and gently fold through the sauce. Transfer to the prepared dish, and top with the potato mash. Bake in the oven for 30 minutes or until heated through and golden brown.

Note: The pie can be made 1–2 days in advance and stored in the fridge. Be sure to bring the pie back to room temperature before cooking.

Who doesn't love a good sausage roll? Ours is the perfect combination of flavoursome pork, stewed apple and sage with our buttery, flaky pastry. A must-have with our Old-fashioned Tomato Sauce!

OLD-FASHIONED PORK SAUSAGE ROLLS

Makes 12 • **Preparation time** 30 minutes plus cooling time • **Cooking time** 40 minutes

Preheat the oven to 180°C (350°F). Line a baking tray with baking paper.

In a medium frying pan, heat the oil over medium–high heat. Add the onion and cook for 5 minutes, until soft and translucent. Add the sage and cook for a further 2 minutes. Remove from the heat and allow to cool.

Place the onion and sage in a large mixing bowl. Add the remaining filling ingredients and mix by hand until combined.

On a lightly floured surface, roll out the pastry into a large rectangle 3 mm (⅛ inch) in thickness. Cut lengthways into two long rectangles.

Roll half the filling mixture into sausage shapes with your hands and place along the edge of one of the pastry sheets. Brush along one edge with the egg wash and fold the pastry over to enclose the sausage meat, sealing the edges together. Repeat with the remaining filling and pastry sheet.

Cut into whatever size you prefer, then space them 3 cm (1¼ inches) apart on the prepared tray. Bake for approximately 25–30 minutes or until golden brown.

Serve with our Old-fashioned Tomato Sauce.

Note: You can use tinned cooked apple.

FILLING
2 tablespoons vegetable oil
2 brown onions, finely diced
1½ bunches (½ cup) sage leaves, picked and chopped
500 g (1 lb 2 oz) minced (ground) pork
500 g (1 lb 2 oz) pork sausage meat
250 g (9 oz) cooked apple, puréed
100 g (3½ oz) dry breadcrumbs
1 egg
salt and pepper

1 quantity Pie Top (see page 219)
egg wash (beat 1 egg yolk with 2 tablespoons thin (pouring) cream)
Old-fashioned Tomato Sauce (see page 229), to serve

CHAPTER № 9

SANDWICHES

No matter when the craving strikes, these combos promise to satisfy every time. Be creative and think outside the sandwich box. The crucial golden rules of sandwich making are to use quality bread and to balance the textures and flavours.

This is our twist on a French classic: a glorified ham and cheese toastie, using good quality ham, eggs and gruyère, smothered in aïoli and toasted until the cheese is oozing and the bread has turned a deep golden brown. It's our top-selling breakfast toastie and a great hangover cure!

CROQUE MADAME

Makes four sandwiches • **Preparation time** 20 minutes • **Cooking time** 10 minutes

Place the slices of bread on your work surface, buttered side down. Spread liberally with aïoli, then place slices of ham and a fried egg on 4 of the bread slices. Finish off with 2 slices of cheese and sandwich together with the remaining slices of bread, buttered side out.

Place in a preheated sandwich press and cook until golden brown and the cheese has melted, approximately 5 minutes.

Serve hot.

8 thick slices of white bread, buttered
60 g (2¼ oz/¼ cup) Aïoli (see page 230)
400 g (14 oz) thinly sliced ham
4 eggs, at room temperature, fried
8 slices gruyère cheese

Roasted eggplant tossed in a tangy vinaigrette and sweetened with sultanas and fresh mint gives a sweet and sour contrast to this hearty vegetarian sandwich.

Without the bread it makes a great antipasto, or serve with our slow-roasted lamb shoulder (see page 214) for a mouth-watering feast.

ROAST EGGPLANT SALAD, FETA, ROAST CAPSICUM MAYO AND ROCKET

80 ml (2½ fl oz/⅓ cup) olive oil
salt and pepper

ROAST EGGPLANT SALAD
2 eggplants (aubergines), diced
1 spring onion (scallion), thinly sliced
45 g (1½ oz/¼ cup) sultanas
  (golden raisins), chopped
1 bunch (½ cup) flat-leaf (Italian)
  parsley, roughly chopped
½ bunch (¼ cup) mint, leaves picked
  and chopped
80 ml (2½ fl oz/⅓ cup) Vinaigrette
  (see page 230)

ROAST CAPSICUM MAYONNAISE
2 red capsicums (peppers), halved
  and seeded
250 g (9 oz/1 cup) Aïoli (see page 230)
a few drops of Tabasco sauce
salt and pepper

salted butter, at room temperature,
  for spreading
8 slices sourdough bread
2 handfuls baby rocket (arugula)
  leaves
150 g (5½ oz) feta cheese, crumbled

Makes four sandwiches • **Preparation time** 30 minutes plus cooling time • **Cooking time** 20 minutes for roasting eggplant and capsicum

Line two baking trays with baking paper. Toss the eggplants and capsicums in two separate bowls with 2 tablespoons of oil in each. Season both well with salt and pepper. Place on the prepared trays and roast for 15–20 minutes or until tender. Allow to cool.

For the roast eggplant salad: Combine the roasted eggplant, spring onion, sultanas, parsley, mint and vinaigrette in a bowl and season well. Lightly toss all the ingredients together.

For the capsicum mayonnaise: Peel the roasted capsicum and purée in a food processor until smooth, blend in the aïoli and Tabasco sauce and season well.

To assemble the sandwiches: Butter the bread. Spread 4 slices of the buttered bread liberally with the capsicum mayo, top with some rocket, then eggplant salad and crumble over the feta to finish. Top with the 4 remaining slices of buttered bread.

Layered with corned beef, heaped with tangy sauerkraut, creamy Russian dressing and molten Swiss cheese, the Reuben is so hypnotically good it has left a lasting impression on us. This is our version of the New York deli classic.

REUBEN

Makes four sandwiches • **Preparation time** 30 minutes • **Cooking time** 2 hours 20 minutes for corned beef

To cook the corned beef, place the silverside in a medium saucepan, add the remaining ingredients and cover with water. Bring slowly to the boil, then reduce to a simmer and cook for 2 hours or until the silverside is tender. Remove from the saucepan, cool and slice thinly.

For the Russian dressing: Put all the ingredients into a food processor and process until blended, but not too smooth. You will need 185 ml (6 fl oz/¾ cup).

To assemble the sandwiches: Butter the bread. Spread 4 slices of the buttered bread liberally with the Russian dressing, top with generous amounts of corned beef, layer over some sauerkraut and finish with the cheese and the 4 remaining slices of bread, buttered sides out. Place in a preheated sandwich press and cook until golden brown and the cheese has melted, approximately 5 minutes.

Serve hot.

Note: The remaining unsliced corned beef can be stored, covered in its cooking liquor, in an airtight container in the fridge for up to 1 week.

CORNED BEEF

1.5 kg (3 lb 5 oz) corned silverside

3 fresh bay leaves

5 garlic cloves, bruised

3 allspice berries

1 onion, halved

1 carrot, halved

2 celery stalks, cut in half

10 black peppercorns

RUSSIAN DRESSING

250 g (9 oz/1 cup) Aïoli (see page 230)

60 ml (2 fl oz/¼ cup) tomato sauce (ketchup)

1 spring onion (scallion), finely chopped

10 cornichons (gherkins), roughly chopped

1 tablespoon bottled horseradish

1 teaspoon Worcestershire sauce

a few drops of Tabasco sauce

salted butter, at room temperature, for spreading

8 slices rye sourdough bread

200 g (7 oz/1 cup) sauerkraut

12 slices Swiss cheese

We all know chicken is a crowd pleaser and this chicken roulade is the star of this sandwich. A lot of time and preparation goes into this sandwich filling, but it is definitely worth the effort. If you are time-poor, use a store-bought roasted, seasoned chicken, making sure it's good quality.

ROAST CHICKEN WITH SAGE AND ONION STUFFING, TOMATO, ROCKET AND MAYO

1.6 kg (3 lb 8 oz) free-range chicken, deboned (this size chicken will make more than 4 sandwiches and will keep in the fridge for 3 days)

STUFFING

100 g (3½ oz) butter

1 onion, finely chopped

1 garlic clove, minced

300 g (10½ oz) sourdough bread

½ bunch (¼ cup) sage, leaves picked and chopped

1 egg, at room temperature, lightly beaten

2 tablespoons milk

olive oil, to brush

salt and pepper

salted butter, at room temperature, for spreading

8 slices sourdough bread

125 g (4½ oz/½ cup) Aïoli (see page 230)

2 ripe tomatoes, sliced

2 handfuls rocket (arugula) leaves

Makes four sandwiches • **Preparation time** 40 minutes plus cooling time • **Cooking time** 45 minutes

For the stuffing: Melt the butter in a small frying pan over medium heat, add the onion and garlic and cook, stirring, for approximately 5 minutes, or until they soften.

Pulse the bread coarsely in a food processor and put in a medium bowl. Add the cooked onion and garlic, then the sage and combine well. Add the egg and gradually add enough of the milk so the mixture is soft and firm, but not too wet. Mix well.

Preheat the oven to 180°C (350°F). Place the boned chicken skin side down on your work surface, and press on the stuffing to form a log on top of the chicken. Roll the chicken (basically fold in half). Tuck in the ends and secure with wooden skewers, and tie the chicken with kitchen string to ensure the shape is even. Brush the chicken with olive oil and season well with salt and pepper. Place on a baking tray, seam side down and roast for 45 minutes. Cool and slice.

To assemble the sandwiches: Butter the bread. Spread 4 slices of the buttered bread liberally with aïoli, top with sliced chicken and tomatoes, season well and finish with rocket. Top with the 4 remaining slices of buttered bread.

A hot, gooey, melty cheese sandwich is as basic as it gets, but this doesn't mean this classic comfort food can't be elevated by using topnotch ingredients. We use a good quality gruyère and home-made Bread 'n' Butter Pickles. It is well worth the effort to make your own pickles — you'll be shocked at how easy it is.

CHEESE TOASTIES

Makes four sandwiches • **Preparation time** 30 minutes plus 3 hours standing time for pickles • **Cooking time** 15 minutes

For the pickles: Wash and thinly slice the cucumbers and onion. Place in a medium bowl, add the salt and 500 ml (17 fl oz/2 cups) cold water. Let stand at room temperature for 3 hours. Drain thoroughly without rinsing.

In a large saucepan, combine the remaining pickle ingredients and bring to the boil, then add the cucumber and onion. Take off the heat, allow to cool, then store in the fridge in an airtight container.

To assemble the cheese toasties: Butter the bread. Place the slices of bread on your work surface, buttered side down. Place the slices of cheese on 4 of the bread slices, top with 250 ml (9 fl oz/1 cup) drained pickles and sandwich together with the remaining slices of bread, buttered side out. Place in a preheated sandwich press and cook until golden brown and the cheese has melted, approximately 5 minutes.

Serve hot.

Note: The pickles will keep in the fridge for 1 month. They're very handy – you can serve them with cheese or cold cuts.

BREAD 'N' BUTTER PICKLES
2 telegraph (long) cucumbers

1 brown onion

2 tablespoons salt

450 ml (15¾ fl oz) white wine vinegar

370 g (13 oz/1⅔ cups) caster (superfine) sugar

1 teaspoon ground turmeric

½ teaspoon mustard seeds

¼ teaspoon celery seeds

salted butter, at room temperature, for spreading

8 slices sourdough bread

12 slices gruyère cheese

THE COOK AND BAKER

The freshness of the crisp apple and tarragon slaw balances the rich flavours of the roasted pork. Lightly toasted, this sandwich is amazing. A great sandwich to use up left-over pork from Sunday's roast.

ROAST PORK, APPLE SLAW AND ROCKET

1 tablespoon minced garlic

1 tablespoon fennel seeds, ground

80 ml (2½ fl oz/⅓ cup) olive oil

½ shoulder of pork, approximately
   750 g (1 lb 10 oz), boned, skinned
   and rolled

salt and pepper

APPLE SLAW

2 granny smith apples, peeled,
   cored and grated

1 spring onion (scallion), thinly sliced

½ bunch (¼ cup) flat-leaf (Italian)
   parsley, finely chopped

2 tablespoons tarragon,
   finely chopped

125 g (4½ oz/½ cup) Aïoli
   (see page 230)

salt and pepper

2 handfuls rocket (arugula) leaves

salted butter, at room temperature,
   for spreading

8 slices sourdough bread

Makes four sandwiches • **Preparation time** 40 minutes plus cooling time • **Cooking time** 1 hour

Preheat the oven to 180°C (350°F). In a small bowl, combine the garlic, fennel seeds and oil, and mix to a paste. Put the prepared pork in a roasting tin. Lather the paste all over the pork, season well and roast for 45–60 minutes. Cool, then slice thinly.

For the apple slaw: Combine all the slaw ingredients in a medium bowl and season well.

To assemble the sandwiches: Butter the bread. On 4 slices of the buttered bread lay generous amounts of roasted pork. Spread over the apple slaw, then add the rocket, and top with the 4 remaining slices of buttered bread.

THE COOK AND BAKER

THE COOK AND BAKER

We stay close to tradition with these small, compact, savoury sandwiches, and use bread straight from the supermarket, good ol' white and brown, sandwich-sliced. Be generous with the fillings — spread right to the edges before removing the crusts. Be sure to have plenty of moistened paper towel or cloths on hand to keep the bread covered and fresh.

EGG AND CHIVE FINGER SANDWICHES

8 free-range eggs, hard boiled

125 g (4½ oz/½ cup) Aïoli
(see page 230)

2 tablespoons finely chopped chives

salt and pepper

salted butter, at room temperature,
for spreading

12 slices white or wholemeal bread,
sandwich slice

Makes 12 ribbons/fingers • **Preparation time** 20 minutes • **Cooking time** nil

Peel and coarsely grate or crumble the eggs into a bowl. Mix with the aïoli and chives and season well with salt and pepper to taste. Butter the bread slices, then lay out 4 slices and spread generously with half the filling. Top with another slice of bread, spread with the remaining filling and finish with another slice of bread.

Remove the crusts and cut each square into thirds to make 3 fingers.

Note: You can make this into curried-egg finger sandwiches by adding 1 teaspoon curry powder to the aïoli mix.

SMOKED SALMON, DILL AND CAPER
FINGER SANDWICHES

Makes 12 ribbons/fingers • **Preparation time** 20 minutes • **Cooking time** nil

In a small bowl, mix together the dill, spring onion and capers. Butter the bread, lay out 4 slices and top with the smoked salmon, then season with pepper. Top with another slice of bread. Spread generously with the cream cheese and then the dill caper salsa and finish with another slice of bread.

Remove the crusts and cut each square into thirds to make 3 fingers.

½ bunch (2 tablespoons) dill,
  finely chopped
1 spring onion (scallion),
  finely chopped
1 tablespoon baby capers,
  drained and chopped
salted butter, at room temperature,
  for spreading
12 slices white or wholemeal bread,
  sandwich slice
250 g (9 oz) smoked salmon
freshly ground black pepper
125 g (4½ oz) light cream cheese,
  at room temperature

CHICKEN AND MAYO FINGER SANDWICHES

2 boneless, skinless chicken breasts

2 fresh bay leaves

2 thyme sprigs

1 garlic clove, smashed

1 celery stalk, finely diced

1 small spring onion (scallion),
finely diced

1 teaspoon fennel seeds, lightly
toasted and ground

250 g (9 oz/1 cup) Aïoli
(see page 230)

salt and pepper

salted butter, at room temperature,
for spreading

12 slices white or wholemeal bread,
sandwich slice

Makes 12 ribbons/fingers • **Preparation time** 20 minutes plus cooling time • **Cooking time** 12 minutes for poaching chicken

Place the chicken breasts in a medium saucepan, add the bay leaves, thyme and garlic and just cover with cold water. Place the pan over medium–high heat, bring the water to the boil, then reduce the heat to low and simmer until cooked, approximately 8–12 minutes depending on the thickness of the breasts. Remove the chicken from the poaching liquid and allow to cool. Discard the bay leaves, thyme and garlic. Chop the chicken finely.

Combine the chicken, celery, spring onion, fennel seeds and aïoli and season well with salt and pepper. Butter the bread slices, then lay out 4 slices and spread generously with half the filling. Top with another slice of bread, spread with the remaining filling and finish with another slice of bread.

Remove the crusts and cut each square into thirds to make 3 fingers.

Note: The remaining chicken stock can be used for sauces, soups or can be frozen for up to 1 month.

Quality lamb and slow cooking are both crucial to the success of this sandwich. This sandwich is inspired by the flavours and aromas of the Middle East.

SLOW-ROASTED LAMB SHOULDER, ROAST CARROTS, LABNE AND MINT

Makes four sandwiches • **Preparation time** 30 minutes plus overnight draining time for labne • **Cooking time** 2 hours 30 minutes

For the labne: Spoon the yoghurt into a sieve lined with a piece of muslin (cheesecloth). Set the sieve over a bowl, cover and place in the fridge overnight to drain.

For the lamb: Preheat the oven to 220°C (425°F). In a small bowl, combine the cumin, garlic, olive oil, salt and pepper, and mix to a paste. Make a few shallow slashes on the fat side of the lamb and rub the cumin paste all over.

Put the prepared lamb in a roasting tin and roast for 30 minutes. Add 250 ml (9 fl oz/1 cup) water and wrap the lamb securely with foil, then turn the oven down to 160°C (315°F) and cook for a further 2 hours or until the meat is falling off the bone. Remove from the oven. Shred the lamb when cool enough to handle.

For the carrots: Line a baking tray with baking paper. In a small bowl, combine the cumin, coriander, olive oil, salt and pepper, and mix to a paste. Toss the carrots in the paste, then spread them over the prepared tray. Roast in the oven with the lamb for the last 30 minutes, until soft and golden brown. When cool, toss through the chopped mint.

To assemble the sandwiches: Butter the bread. Spread 4 slices of the buttered bread liberally with the labne, and top with the lamb, carrots and apple and mint jam. Season well and finish with the 4 remaining slices of buttered bread.

LABNE

500 g (1 lb 2 oz) Greek-style yoghurt

SLOW-ROASTED LAMB

1 tablespoon ground cumin

1 tablespoon minced garlic

2 tablespoons olive oil

salt and pepper

1 shoulder of lamb, approximately 1 kg (2 lb 4 oz), bone in

ROAST CARROTS

2 teaspoons ground cumin

½ teaspoon ground coriander

2 tablespoons olive oil

salt and pepper

500 g (1 lb 2 oz) carrots, cut into 1.5 cm (⅝ inch) slices

½ bunch (¼ cup) fresh mint leaves, picked and chopped

salted butter, at room temperature, for spreading

8 slices sourdough bread

4 tablespoons Apple and Mint Jam (see page 227)

salt and pepper

CHAPTER №10

BASE
RECIPES

The following recipes are the bricks
and mortar of The Cook and Baker,
and we use them daily. In no time at all
you will find that these versatile recipes
have become an essential part
of your repertoire.

SWEET PASTRY

Makes about 500 g (1 lb 2 oz) • **Preparation time** 15 minutes plus 30–60 minutes chilling time • **Cooking time** nil

Sift the flour, sugar and salt into the bowl of an electric mixer fitted with a paddle attachment. Add the cold butter and mix on low speed until it resembles fine breadcrumbs.

Add the water and mix until the dough forms a ball. Transfer the dough to a lightly floured work surface, press into a flat disc, then wrap in plastic wrap. Refrigerate for 30–60 minutes before using.

Note: Keeps in the fridge for 3 days or can be frozen for up to 1 month.

250 g (9 oz/1⅔ cups) plain (all-purpose) flour
55 g (2 oz/¼ cup) caster (superfine) sugar
pinch of salt
200 g (7 oz) butter, cold and diced
50 ml (1¾ fl oz) cold water

PIE BASE (SHORTCRUST)

Makes about 500 g (1 lb 2 oz) • **Preparation time** 15 minutes plus 30 minutes–overnight refrigeration • **Cooking time** nil

A basic pastry that is made with about half the usual quantity of fat to flour and has a crisp but crumbly texture.

In the bowl of an electric mixer fitted with a paddle attachment, place the flour, butter and salt. Mix on low speed until it resembles breadcrumbs. Add the cold water, and mix until a dough is formed.

Remove from the bowl. Roll into a ball and flatten, wrap with plastic wrap and refrigerate for 30 minutes or overnight.

Note: Keeps in the fridge for 3 days or can be frozen for up to 1 month.

300 g (10½ oz/2 cups) plain (all-purpose) flour
150 g (5½ oz) butter, cold and diced
½ teaspoon salt
125 ml (4 fl oz/½ cup) cold water

PIE TOP (ROUGH PUFF)

350 g (12 oz/2⅓ cups) plain
   (all-purpose) flour
¼ teaspoon salt
335 g (11¾ oz) butter, cold and cubed
140 ml (4¾ fl oz) cold water

Makes about 750 g (1 lb 10 oz) • **Preparation time** 40 minutes plus 30 minutes–overnight chilling plus another 2 hours chilling time • **Cooking time** nil

A light flaky pastry similar to a full puff pastry without the hard work.

In the bowl of an electric mixer fitted with a paddle attachment, place the flour, salt and 135 g (4¾ oz) of the butter. Mix on low speed until it resembles coarse breadcrumbs. Add the remaining butter, and mix on low until the butter cubes are coated with the flour. (You still want to see big cubes of butter.) Add the cold water and mix on low, until the dough comes together. Add a little extra water if needed.

Remove from the bowl, press into a rough rectangular shape, wrap with plastic wrap and refrigerate for at least 30 minutes or overnight.

Lightly flour your work surface. Roll the dough out to a 25 x 60 cm (10 x 24 inch) rectangle, then with the long side facing you, fold in the two ends to meet in the middle. Then fold them over again. This is called a bookend fold. Rest in the fridge for at least 30 minutes.

Lightly flour your work surface, and place the rested dough on it with the short end facing you. Roll it again lengthways to 20 x 50 cm (8 x 20 inches). Then, with the long side facing you, fold as before. Rest for another 30 minutes and repeat this step for a third time. Rest in the fridge for at least 1 hour prior to using.

Notes: The longer you rest your pastry between folds the flakier it will be. Left over trimmings should be stacked up and chilled before re-rolling for another use – do not scrunch them together in a ball or you will lose the layers. Keeps in the fridge for 3 days or can be frozen for up to 1 month.

PIZZA DOUGH

Makes about 1.2 kg (2 lb 10 oz) • **Preparation time** 20 minutes plus 30 minutes proving time for dough

Place the flour, dried yeast, sugar and salt in the bowl of an electric mixer fitted with a dough hook attachment. Add the tepid water and oil and mix on low speed until combined. Knead the dough at this speed for approximately 5 minutes or until smooth and elastic.

Remove the bowl from the mixer, cover with plastic wrap and set aside in a warm place until the dough doubles in size, approximately 30 minutes.

Remove the dough from the bowl and place on a lightly floured surface. Knead for 30 seconds until the dough is its original size. Shape the dough into a ball, and press lightly to flatten.

Note: You can store the dough in the fridge for up to 3 days or freeze it for up to 1 month. Make sure the dough is returned to room temperature before using it.

750 g (1 lb 10 oz/5 cups) plain (all-purpose) flour
40 g (1½ oz) dried yeast
¼ teaspoon caster (superfine) sugar
¼ teaspoon salt
400 ml (14 fl oz) tepid water
2 tablespoons olive oil

CUSTARD FILLING (SAVOURY)

6 eggs, at room temperature
400 ml (14 fl oz) thin (pouring) cream
salt and pepper
freshly grated nutmeg

Makes about 750 ml (26 fl oz/3 cups) • **Preparation time** 10 minutes • **Cooking time** nil

Using a hand whisk, beat the eggs, cream, salt, pepper and nutmeg together in a medium bowl until well incorporated.

Note: This lasts in the fridge 3–4 days, so can be made in advance.

VANILLA WHIPPED CREAM

½ vanilla bean
300 ml (10½ fl oz) thin (pouring) cream
1 tablespoon caster (superfine) sugar

Makes about 500 ml (17 fl oz/2 cups) • **Preparation time** 10 minutes • **Cooking time** nil

Split the half vanilla bean lengthways, then scrape the seeds using the tip of a sharp knife.

Combine the cream, vanilla seeds and sugar in a bowl and use an electric mixer with a whisk attachment to whisk the cream until it forms soft peaks.

Note: Cover and store in the fridge for up to 1 day.

VANILLA PASTRY CRÈME

Makes about 650 ml (22½ fl oz) • **Preparation time** 20 minutes • **Cooking time** 30 minutes

We use whole eggs, which makes for a lighter pastry crème.

Split the half vanilla bean lengthways, then scrape the seeds using the tip of a sharp knife.

In a heavy-based saucepan over medium heat, put the milk, salt, vanilla bean and seeds. Bring slowly to the boil. Remove the saucepan from the heat as soon as it reaches boiling point.

While waiting for the milk to boil, in a large bowl whisk together the cornflour and sugar, then add the eggs and whisk until smooth. Pour half the hot milk onto the eggs and sugar, whisking well. Pour in the remaining milk and whisk again.

Strain this mixture into a clean heavy-based saucepan and cook over medium heat, whisking constantly until the custard is very thick, approximately 10–15 minutes.

Remove from the heat. Whisk the butter into the custard until smooth and incorporated. Pour the pastry crème into a bowl. Cover with plastic wrap directly on the custard to prevent a skin forming on the surface. Leave to cool completely before using.

Note: Keep in an airtight container in the fridge for up to 5 days.

VARIATION

For Chocolate Pastry Crème: Add 80 g (2¾ oz) dark chocolate, finely chopped, when whisking the butter into the custard.

½ vanilla bean

500 ml (17 fl oz/2 cups) full-cream milk

¼ teaspoon salt

60 g (2¼ oz/½ cup) cornflour (cornstarch)

110 g (3¾ oz/½ cup) caster (superfine) sugar

2 eggs, at room temperature

60 g (2¼ oz) butter, diced

DIPLOMAT CRÈME

650 ml (22½ fl oz) chilled Vanilla
or Chocolate Pastry Crème
(see page 222)
300 ml (10½ fl oz) thin (pouring)
cream, whipped

Makes 950 ml (33½ fl oz) • **Preparation time** 10 minutes • **Cooking time** nil

Diplomat crème is a lighter version of pastry crème. Basically, it is pastry crème with added plain, whipped cream mixed through.

Loosen the chilled pastry crème by whisking in a bowl until smooth. Gently fold the whipped cream through the pastry crème. Cover with plastic wrap directly on the diplomat crème to prevent a skin forming on the surface.

Note: Store in an airtight container. Keeps for 3–4 days refrigerated.

SALTED CARAMEL

495 g (1 lb ½ oz/2¼ cups) caster
(superfine) sugar
1 teaspoon sea salt
100 g (3½ oz) butter, diced
65 g (2¼ oz/¼ cup) sour cream
70 ml (2¼ fl oz) thin (pouring) cream

Makes about 750 ml (26 fl oz/3 cups) • **Preparation time** 20 minutes • **Cooking time** 20 minutes

Place the sugar and 150 ml (5 fl oz) water in a large heavy-based saucepan. Without stirring, cook over low heat to dissolve the sugar, approximately 5 minutes.

Increase the heat to high and boil the sugar until it turns golden caramel in colour. Swirl it occasionally just to even out the colour and keep the hot spots from burning. Once the colour starts to change, watch your caramel very closely as it can go from undercooked to overcooked within a few seconds.

Remove from the heat and very carefully add the butter, sour cream and cream, whisking until the butter has melted and the caramel is smooth. Allow to cool completely.

Note: Store in an airtight container in the fridge for up to 1 month.

CRÈME ANGLAISE

Makes about 1.5 litres (52 fl oz/6 cups) • **Preparation time** 20 minutes • **Cooking time** 20 minutes

Split the vanilla bean in half lengthways, then scrape the seeds from the halves using the tip of a sharp knife.

In a heavy-based saucepan, pour in the milk, 250 ml (9 fl oz/1 cup) of the cream and the vanilla bean and seeds. Place over medium heat and bring slowly to the boil. Remove the saucepan from the heat as soon as it reaches boiling point.

While the milk, cream and vanilla are heating, whisk together the egg yolks and sugar in a bowl until smooth. Pour half the hot milk and cream mixture onto the eggs and sugar, whisking well as you do so. Pour in the remaining milk and cream mixture and whisk again.

Pour this mixture back into the saucepan and cook over medium heat, stirring constantly until the mixture coats the back of the spoon, approximately 5 minutes. Remove from the heat, then stir through the remaining 250 ml (9 fl oz/1 cup) of cream to stop the cooking process.

Cool, then strain through a sieve into a container and cover with plastic wrap directly on the crème anglaise to prevent a skin forming on the surface.

Note: Store in the fridge for up to 7 days. The egg whites can be frozen for later use or can be used to make the Pavlova Wreath (see page 136) or Meringue (see page 62).

1 vanilla bean
500 ml (17 fl oz/2 cups) full cream milk
500 ml (17 fl oz/2 cups) thin (pouring) cream
12 egg yolks, at room temperature
165 g (5¾ oz/¾ cup) caster (superfine) sugar

MANDARIN MARMALADE

1.25 kg (2 lb 12 oz) mandarins
735 g (1 lb 10 oz/3⅓ cups) caster
    (superfine) sugar
juice of 1 lemon

Makes about 1.5 kg (3 lb 5 oz/4⅔ cups) • **Preparation time** 45 minutes plus 10 minutes standing time • **Cooking time** 45 minutes

Peel the mandarins, trying to keep the peel as whole as possible. Cut the peel into thin strips and set aside.

Cut the mandarins in half horizontally and remove the seeds. Wrap the seeds tightly in a piece of muslin (cheesecloth) and tie with kitchen string. Roughly chop the flesh of the mandarins and place in a large heavy-based saucepan with the peel, sugar, lemon juice and 1 litre (35 fl oz/4 cups) water. Add the seeds in the muslin.

Stir constantly over low heat until the sugar is dissolved, for approximately 5 minutes. Bring to the boil, then reduce the heat to medium. Simmer uncovered, without stirring, for approximately 30 minutes or until the mixture will jell when tested on a cold saucer. Discard the muslin parcel. Stand the marmalade for 10 minutes before pouring into hot sterilised jars.

Jelling test: Drop a teaspoon of mixture onto a saucer that has been chilled in the freezer. Return to the freezer for a few minutes. If jelled it will have formed a skin that wrinkles when pushed with a finger.

To sterilise jars: Clean jars with hot soapy water, rinse well, then drain and place on a baking tray and put into a 120°C (250°F) oven for 20 minutes until they are fully dried.

Note: Store in a cool, dark place for up to 12 months. Once opened, keep in the fridge and use within 1 month.

RASPBERRY JAM

Makes about 1.25 kg (2 lb 12 oz/4 cups) • **Preparation time** 30 minutes plus 10 minutes standing time • **Cooking time** 40 minutes

1 vanilla bean
1 kg (2 lb 4 oz/8 cups) raspberries, fresh or frozen
495 g (1 lb 1½ oz/2¼ cups) caster (superfine) sugar
juice of 1 lemon

Split the vanilla bean in half lengthways, then scrape the seeds from the halves using the tip of a sharp knife.

In a heavy-based saucepan, put the raspberries, sugar, lemon juice, vanilla bean and seeds, and 125 ml (4 fl oz/½ cup) water. Stir constantly over low heat until the sugar is dissolved, approximately 5 minutes.

Bring to the boil, then reduce the heat. Simmer uncovered, stirring occasionally, for approximately 20–25 minutes until the mixture will jell when tested on a cold saucer (see page 225).

Discard the vanilla bean. Stand the jam for 10 minutes to settle before pouring into hot sterilised jars (see page 225).

Note: Store in a cool, dark place for up to 12 months. Once opened, keep in the fridge and use within 1 month.

BERRY JAM

Makes about 1.25 kg (2 lb 12 oz/4 cups) • **Preparation time** 30 minutes plus 10 minutes standing time • **Cooking time** 40 minutes

1 vanilla bean
1 kg (2 lb 4 oz) mixed berries (raspberries, blueberries, blackberries), fresh or frozen
495 g (1 lb 1½ oz/2¼ cups) caster (superfine) sugar
juice of 1 lemon

Split the vanilla bean in half lengthways, then scrape the seeds from the halves using the tip of a sharp knife.

In a heavy-based saucepan, put the berries, sugar, lemon juice, vanilla bean and seeds, and 125 ml (4 fl oz/½ cup) water. Stir constantly over low heat until the sugar is dissolved, approximately 5 minutes.

Bring to the boil, then reduce the heat. Simmer uncovered, stirring occasionally, for approximately 20–25 minutes until the mixture will jell when tested on a cold saucer (see page 225).

Discard the vanilla bean. Stand the jam for 10 minutes to settle before pouring into hot sterilised jars (see page 225).

Note: Store in a cool, dark place for up to 12 months. Once opened, keep in the fridge and use within 1 month.

APPLE AND MINT JAM

4 large green apples
4 tablespoons light brown sugar
½ cinnamon stick
2 tablespoons apple cider vinegar
50 g (1¾ oz/1 cup) chopped mint
  leaves
salt and pepper

Makes about 500 g (1 lb 2 oz/1½ cups) • **Preparation time** 20 minutes • **Cooking time** 20 minutes

Peel, core and dice the apples and place in a medium saucepan with the sugar, cinnamon stick and 80 ml (2½ fl oz/⅓ cup) water.

Cover and cook over medium–low heat for 20 minutes or until the apples are soft and falling apart.

Remove from the heat, and take out and discard the cinnamon stick. Stir in the vinegar and mint and season well with salt and pepper.

Note: Refrigerate in sterilised jars (see page 225) or in an airtight container for up to 1 month.

LEMON CURD

Makes about 1.25 g (2 lb 12 oz/5 cups) • **Preparation time** 30 minutes • **Cooking time** 15 minutes

In a large heatproof bowl, whisk together the lemon juice, whole eggs and egg yolks, caster sugar and salt until well combined. Place over a large saucepan of simmering water, and make sure the base of the bowl does not touch the water.

Hand-whisk for approximately 10–15 minutes until the mixture becomes very thick and reaches 82°C (180°F) on a sugar thermometer. Remove the bowl from the saucepan.

Add the butter a little at a time, whisking after each addition and making sure the butter is fully incorporated before adding more.

Lemon curd should be pale yellow and thick.

Note: Refrigerate in sterilised jars (see page 225) or an airtight container for up to 2 weeks.

300 ml (10½ fl oz) lemon juice
6 eggs, at room temperature
2 egg yolks, at room temperature
330 g (11¾ oz/1½ cups) caster (superfine) sugar
¼ teaspoon salt
450 g (1 lb) butter, at room temperature, diced

PASSIONFRUIT CURD

Makes about 1.25 g (2 lb 12 oz/5 cups) • **Preparation time** 30 minutes • **Cooking time** 15 minutes

In a large heatproof bowl, whisk together the passionfruit juice and lemon juice, whole eggs and egg yolks, caster sugar and salt until well combined. Place over a large saucepan of simmering water, and make sure the base of the bowl does not touch the water.

Hand-whisk for approximately 10–15 minutes until the mixture becomes very thick and reaches 82°C (180°F) on a sugar thermometer. Remove the bowl from the saucepan.

Add the butter a little at a time, whisking after each addition and making sure the butter is fully incorporated before adding more.

The curd should be pale yellow and thick.

Note: Refrigerate in sterilised jars (see page 225) or an airtight container for up to 2 weeks.

150 ml (5 fl oz) passionfruit pulp, strained
150 ml (5 fl oz) lemon juice
6 eggs, at room temperature
2 egg yolks, at room temperature
330 g (11¾ oz/1½ cups) caster (superfine) sugar
¼ teaspoon salt
450 g (1 lb) butter, at room temperature, diced

OLD-FASHIONED TOMATO SAUCE

2 kg (4 lb 8 oz) ripe tomatoes,
   coarsely chopped
500 g (1 lb 2 oz) granny smith apples,
   peeled, cored and coarsely
   chopped
500 g (1 lb 2 oz) brown onions,
   coarsely chopped
495 g (1 lb 1½ oz/2⅔ cups, lightly
   packed) light brown sugar
375 ml (13 fl oz/1½ cups) malt vinegar
6 whole cloves
6 allspice berries
1 teaspoon black peppercorns
4 fresh bay leaves
1 tablespoon salt

Makes about 2.5 litres (87 fl oz/10 cups) • **Preparation time** 30 minutes •
Cooking time 1 hour 15 minutes

In a large heavy-based saucepan combine all the ingredients. Slowly
bring to the boil over medium–high heat, stirring to dissolve the sugar.
   Reduce to a simmer and cook uncovered for 1 hour.
   Pass the sauce through a fine mouli and check the seasoning.

Note: Pour into hot sterilised jars or bottles (see page 225) or keep in an
airtight container in the fridge for up to 1 month.

CARAMELISED ONION

2 tablespoons olive oil
3 large red or brown onions,
   thinly sliced
¼ teaspoon salt
2 tablespoons light brown sugar
2 tablespoons balsamic vinegar

Makes about 500 g (1 lb 2 oz/2 cups) • **Preparation time** 20 minutes •
Cooking time 30 minutes

Heat the oil in a large deep frying pan over low heat. Add the onions
and salt and cook for 15–20 minutes until softened. Stir frequently to
prevent them from browning.
   When the onion is cooked and lightly golden, stir in the sugar and
vinegar. Continue to cook over low heat for a further 5–10 minutes,
stirring occasionally, until sticky and caramelised.

Note: Use immediately or store in the fridge in a sterilised jar (see
page 225) or airtight container for up to 1 month.

AÏOLI

Makes about 750 g (1 lb 10 oz/3 cups) • **Preparation time** 20 minutes • **Cooking time** nil

In a food processor, place the egg yolks, mustards, garlic, salt and lemon juice, and process until combined.

While blending, pour in the oils in a slow steady stream until emulsified and thick. Check the seasoning.

Add boiling water to thin if necessary.

Note: This can be made in advance and stored in the fridge in an airtight container for up to 1 month.

4 egg yolks, at room temperature
1 tablespoon dijon mustard
1 tablespoon wholegrain mustard
1 garlic clove, chopped
½ teaspoon sea salt flakes, plus extra if needed
juice of ½ lemon
500 ml (17 fl oz/2 cups) vegetable oil
250 ml (9 fl oz/1 cup) olive oil
pepper

VINAIGRETTE

Makes about 330 ml (11¼ fl oz/1⅓ cups) • **Preparation time** 10 minutes • **Cooking time** nil

In a small bowl, whisk together the vinegar, mustard, salt, pepper and sugar. Slowly add the oil, whisking thoroughly until emulsified.

Note: Store refrigerated in a sterilised jar or bottle (see page 225). Keeps for 1 month.

80 ml (2½ fl oz/⅓ cup) white wine vinegar
1 tablespoon dijon mustard
salt and pepper
1 teaspoon caster (superfine) sugar
250 ml (9 fl oz/1 cup) vegetable oil

INDEX

ACKNOWLEDGMENTS

I would like to take this opportunity to thank my business partner, mentor, confidante, BFF, pseudo-wife and fellow baker/chef, Cherie. I am indebted to you for all you have shown me over the past 22 years, professionally and socially. Thank you for believing in me. We have created an unbelievable business together, a place to share, teach, nurture and most of all laugh – we should be extremely proud of ourselves. To my amazing family and friends, I know you haven't seen much of me during the last 3 years, and I thank you for your never-ending support and words of wisdom. **TASS**

My biggest thank you goes to my business partner and long-time best friend, Tass. You have always motivated and inspired me and kept me in love with my profession. To work beside someone every day who has such talent and the same passion as I do is a rarity. I respect you, Tass, and love what we are achieving every day at The Cook and Baker. To my beautiful soul mate, Peggy, thank you for coming into my life. To my daughter, Coco, you have inspired me, and I hope I have taught you that if you believe in something passionately, you succeed; if you work hard towards your goals, they come to fruition. I love you with all my heart. xxx **CHERIE**

Thank you to all our baristas, front of house staff, pastry chefs and our boys in the back kitchen, past and present, for your commitment and professionalism. You have all helped in the success of The Cook and Baker. Special mentions to Troy Holland, Lauren Dearing, Lisa Krebel and Tamasine McNamara, who have worked so tirelessly and enthusiastically, and have set the benchmark – we truly are grateful. Gurvinder (King Harry) Singh, who has been with us from the beginning, your endless energy and dedication never cease to amaze us, you are a living legend.

Thanks to Cheryl Akle, our agent, for your encouragement and for believing in us. To Jane Morrow, Barbara McClenahan, Megan Pigott, Vanessa Pellatt, Jacqui Porter and Dan Peterson and all the team at Murdoch Books for making this book happen. To Chris Chen, whose photography has made this book come alive, and Vanessa Austin, the amazing stylist, for putting up with our pedantic personalities – what a brilliant team!

ACKNOWLEDGMENTS

Published in 2015 by Murdoch Books, an imprint of Allen & Unwin

Murdoch Books Australia
83 Alexander Street
Crows Nest NSW 2065
Phone: +61 (0) 2 8425 0100
Fax: +61 (0) 2 9906 2218
murdochbooks.com.au
info@murdochbooks.com.au

Murdoch Books UK
Erico House, 6th Floor
93–99 Upper Richmond Road
Putney, London SW15 2TG
Phone: +44 (0) 20 8785 5995
murdochbooks.co.uk
info@murdochbooks.co.uk

For Corporate Orders & Custom Publishing contact Noel Hammond,
National Business Development Manager, Murdoch Books Australia

Publisher: Jane Morrow
Editorial Manager: Barbara McClenahan
Design Manager: Megan Pigott
Project Editor: Vanessa Pellatt
Design: Dan Peterson and Jacqui Porter, Northwood Green
Photographer: Chris Chen
Stylist: Vanessa Austin
Food Editor: Michelle Earl
Production Manager: Mary Bjelobrk

A cataloguing-in-publication entry is available from the catalogue of the National Library of Australia at nla.gov.au.

ISBN 978 1 74336 519 9 Australia
ISBN 978 1 74336 528 1 UK

A catalogue record for this book is available from the British Library.

Colour reproduction by Splitting Image Colour Studio Pty Ltd, Clayton, Victoria
Printed by 1010 Printing International Limited, China

IMPORTANT: Those who might be at risk from the effects of salmonella poïsoning (the elderly, pregnant women, young children and those suffering from immune deficiency diseases) should consult their doctor with any concerns about eating raw eggs.

OVEN GUIDE: You may find cooking times vary depending on the oven you are using. For fan-forced ovens, as a general rule, set the oven temperature to 20°C (35°F) lower than indicated in the recipe.

MEASURES GUIDE: We have used 20 ml (4 teaspoon) tablespoon measures. If you are using a 15 ml (3 teaspoon) tablespoon, add an extra teaspoon of the ingredient for each tablespoon specified.